Simply Unapologetic

Annie L. Mendez

"One woman's resilience to recreate a life she now loves."

Simply Unapologetic

Simply Unapologetic

The information contained in this book is based on the life experiences and opinions perceived and expressed by the author.

Published, distributed, and printed in the United States of America by Rose Gold Publishing, LLC.

Names and events contained in this book have been changed to protect the privacy & identity of the characters except for the author, Annie and her son Jeremiah.

ISBN: 978-1-952070-47-1

www.RoseGoldPublishingLLC.com

A Special Thanks...

To my fifth-grade teacher who gave me a failing grade on an essay I poured my heart into writing. He then proceeded to say, "No ten-year-old can write like this." and continued to say, "You must have copied it from a book."

Thank you to my Aunt Lynn for always believing in that little ten-year-old girl. You have always been there for me, and for that I am eternally grateful for.

Special Dedication

Simply Unapologetic, my first book is dedicated to my son Jeremiah. You were my strength in the midst of some of my darkest hours. Your smile and love carried me through more than you will ever know or could possibly comprehend. I couldn't love another human being more than I love you. Thank you for being the most wonderful son a mom could ever ask for. Lastly, thank you for going along with my crazy plans as we changed the course of our lives from one country to another. Love you forever!

"I will not die an unlived life. I will not live in fear of falling or catching fire. I choose to inhabit my days, to allow my living to open me, to make me less afraid, more accessible, to loosen my heart until it becomes a wing, a torch, a promise. I choose to risk my significance: to live so that which comes to me as seed goes to the next as blossom and that which comes to me as blossom, goes on as fruit." - Dawna Markova

"In order to write about life first you must live it." - Ernest Hemingway

Simply Unapologetic

Annie L. Mendez

"One woman's resilience to recreate a life she now loves."

Table of Contents

Chapters

Introduction

Imagine your whole life up until you are thirty-one years old being known as the one with the big smile, always seemingly happy, the one that always made everyone around you laugh. Laughter for me was an escape from my dark reality because the truth of the matter was that behind closed doors I was dying on the inside.

Cycles are hard to break, and little did I know the decade in my twenties would be some of my darkest hours. At the time I didn't realize the poor decisions that I was making by choosing the wrong partners and allowing them to be abusive to me mentally and physically. This ultimately left my soul bleeding to death and having the person I was staring at in the mirror unrecognizable. I also had to do this while bringing a beautiful son in this world and raise him as a single mom.

So, the next question I had to ask myself was how was I

going to stop this vicious cycle of abuse? How was I going to recreate a life of my dreams? How would I live life on my terms freely and unapologetically? Travel the world? Take risks? Live life for me and not some picture of what society said it should look like? How could I give my son a different life? How could I do all the things my soul had been yearning for?

Then as I began to enter the decade into my thirties, "The Secret," The Law of Attraction was introduced into my life! That was the moment when I realized my thoughts were attracting the very thing I did or did not want. I was a walking human magnet sending out signals. The greater the feeling was, the stronger the vibrations that would penetrate into the universe. It was up to me to change my mindset and know that life didn't have to be this way. I could have the life I wanted and live on purpose! I realized my dreams were never too big; it was my thinking that was too small. I suddenly made a choice to recreate my life, and you can, too!

My journey may have started dark, but it certainly doesn't end that way. Through heartbreak, divorce, love, travel, friendships, international dating, and more, it's about ultimately realizing that this journey means sometimes you must take a chance on YOU!

Chapter 1

Happy New Year!

After a devastating breakup via a handwritten letter from my high school/college sweetheart of almost five years, I experienced for the first time a broken heart. Breakups happen and life seems to go on. However, the broken heart is a reminder of the pain that just seemingly won't go away. The thought of jumping right into the next relationship just seemed like the therapeutic thing to do. I wanted to feel alive again and dismiss those achy feelings that kept tugging at my emotions.

Dating as a young and single twenty-year-old adult was fun, confusing, and bewildering all at once. It was a whole new world out there. While on my latest dating adventures, I met a twenty-one-year-old man named Charles at a party I was throwing on Greek

Road. He was a friend of the DJ who was spinning music that evening for my friends and me. Months later he was very persistent with his pursuit to have me go on a date with him. Nevertheless, he said all the right things until I finally caved and said, "Yes." He wasn't my type, but he was very sweet and charming. Within weeks of us dating he told me he loved me. I, on the other hand, didn't respond except to say, "Thank you" followed by a kiss. I know the logical thing to say after one says that to you is to respond back with an I love you, too. I wanted to take things slowly and ensure I could still get my first love out of my mind and heart.

New Year's Eve had come, and we were just seconds from ringing in the New Year! You could hear the crowd at the party shouting......TEN! NINE! EIGHT! SEVEN! SIX! FIVE! FOUR! THREE! TWO! ONE! I whispered softly in Charles ear for the first time, "I love you". I was in love again! He wrapped me in his arms shouting out loud, "My baby loves me! My baby loves me!" He had been longing to hear those words back.

A few weeks into the New Year my first love wanted to meet with me. I mean right after our breakup he vanished off the face of the earth. This came to me as a complete surprise out of the blue so unexpectedly. It was a cold and frigid January when I saw him, and it felt as if I was staring at a ghost. He parked outside my apartment, and we sat in his car. Staring at him as my mind was racing with questions. Was it real? Was he real? Was he really here? A zillion thoughts entered my head. Why did he leave? Does he still love me? Do I love him? Are we getting back together? All the urges to ask all these questions I held back. Remembering how he broke up with me like the scene in the series *Sex in the City* when Berger breaks up with Carrie on a Post-it note. We continued chatting in his car whereas at this point I solely just wanted closure, so I decided to mentally let him go. I was in love now with Charles, but my heart, too, was still undeniably in love with my first. I chose to suppress those feelings for my first love and start to envision a future with Charles.

That summer Charles and I packed a romantic picnic for two and discussed about what our forever together would look like. Weeks later that July in front of the Drake Hotel near a white gazebo on Michigan Avenue, Charles went down on one knee and proposed to me. I was on cloud nine! He was my fiancé, and I couldn't be happier! On Friday, February 13th, (Yes, Friday the 13th!) seven months later we were married. As I walked down the aisle of his sweet mother's church with my dear dad next to me about to give me away as my beautiful mother sat in the front row looking on, there stood my soon-to-be husband who was staring at me with tears streaming down his cheek. As I stood there at the altar in a long beautiful white dress and an intricate veil covering my face, truthfully, I was a terrified twenty-one-year-old internally freaking out! I started really questioning my decision when I was in the limo heading towards the church. Everything was hitting me rapidly. Admittedly, being the hopeless romantic that I am, the only thing that was going through my head was the hope of secretly wanting my first love to suddenly burst through the church doors and yell, "Don't do it! I love you!"

See what I didn't mention was how Charles was being very abusive to me during the course of our dating relationship. I know I should have left then, but he was so good at being sorry. He surely meant it this time, right?

We said our vows and headed to the reception hall laughing, drinking, and dancing the night away. I felt as if the compass of change for the better was angling in our favor. The next morning, we were packed and ready to go on our honeymoon. We were both young and broke---so broke we took the most uncomfortable bus ride from Chicago to the Poconos that was about 24 hours too long. We couldn't afford airplane tickets, and to be fair we didn't care, we were together. We had an incredible honeymoon, and things were finally feeling perfect.

Three months later I was expecting.

Chapter 2

Unrecognizable

I knew the marriage I was in was toxic. I was in love with the fantasy of what I thought our love, our family could be. However, there were more dark days filled with mental and physical abuse that still continued past the I do's. I was about five and a half months pregnant when Charles pushed me down a set of stairs in our home. I had gone to the bathroom and started to bleed and felt something might be wrong. Crying hysterically, I called my childhood friend Marla. She quickly came and drove me to the hospital emergency room to be checked. I kept Qupraying, "God PLEASE! PLEASE! Don't let me lose my baby!" The love and bond I felt for my unborn child was a feeling I can't explain in words. The doctor then asked if I had been physically harmed, and I turned to Marla and just started to cry. I lied to the nurse, but she still gave me a pamphlet about getting help just in case. By the grace of God, I didn't lose my baby, but I will never forget the feeling of thinking I might have. I never once took for granted the privilege and honor of being blessed to carry my baby full term.

Why did I continue to think I could change Charles? Save him and rescue him from self-destruction? See Charles had a very common disease, one I like to call the Dr. Jekyll and Mr. Hyde personality syndrome.

He had a calm, soft, and gentle demeanor about him. He was most definitely the shy and quiet type, opposite of me. Time went on, and his other side started to emerge. He was the complete opposite, very ice-cold, non-sensitive, and angry type of guy now. Had I seen the signs before I got married? Yes, many signs! Time and time again there were red blinking lights! I told myself, "But he loves me!" "No, really he does!" Hello!!!!! I wish I could have shaken that twenty-year-old and said, "Wake up!!!" "Love doesn't hurt!" Instead, all I did was convince myself that he would change and that he really does love me.

He continued to be abusive physically and mentally to me. He would demean me in such a way that I felt so disgusted with myself. I remember looking in the mirror crying and saying, "Why am I so ugly?" This beautiful girl saw nothing but disgust. This man's words plastered all over my body like an invisible permanent tattoo with a lingering ink consisting of mental pain to continuously remind me. I started truly to believe what he was saying to me. I started feeling such incredible shame.

I couldn't see it at the time, but boy, how I wish I realized then that anyone who is being verbally abusive is really unmasking all of their own insecurities about them and mirroring how they feel about themselves. Mental abuse is like taking doses of poisonous venom to destroy your soul.

I know that the first time it happened to me, I felt nothing but complete and utter shock! I vowed something like this would never happen to me, or I could change the circumstance especially growing up in that type of atmosphere. Yet, I still felt the need to still compromise and fill my head with all these excuses:

"We have more good times than bad!"

"He only does it once in a while!"

"I can't afford to live on my own!"

"He really loves me!"

"He is really sorry!"

I tried to convince myself it's not that bad. The bottom line, wrong is wrong, and my past has shown that if he hit me once, he will hit me again and again.

The verbal abuse I was experiencing was profoundly painful. I knew deep down that to think that mental abuse is any better would be ludicrous. Mental abuse is a slow and terrible death to your internal thinking and being. I knew I could never feel alive being in that type of situation. Day after day of hearing you are so awful, and disgusting is so damaging. I knew I had to get out of that type of toxicity!

A few months later, while I was eight months pregnant,

Charles and I got into a quarrel. He got so upset he took his fist and punched me in the face asking me if I wanted his fist to move downward so he might "accidentally" strike somewhere else. All I could do was hold my pregnant belly and wobble as quickly as possible to the bathroom so I could lock the door. There I was on the bathroom floor, sobbing as I grasped my pregnant belly tightly. I kept telling my unborn baby while rubbing my belly, "I will always protect you no matter what". I was due on Super Bowl Sunday, and I, being a sports fanatic, loved the idea of how exciting it would be to possibly go into labor on that day. When I reminded Charles of this possibility, he reminded me that he was still going to be watching the football game with his friends. Our first child, and that was his response. Saturday night, the night before the big American football game and the eve of my due date, Charles never came home. My dear friend Sona stayed with me that evening rubbing my back and consoling me. How grateful I was for her being there for me. She left that morning after ensuring I had packed my overnight bag for the hospital "just in case". I was having some stomach cramping but didn't think much about it. I headed over to Subway to get a six-foot turkey sandwich with a mountain of juicy pickles on it. As I was heading back home, suddenly the pain became more and more intense. My childhood best friend Yana and godmother to my unborn son arrived shortly thereafter at my door with her boyfriend. Yana exclaimed, "You are in labor!"

I quickly responded, "No, I am not!" I mean everyone said you would know, but I thought perhaps it was stomach pain from the burrito I had the night before. Yana insisted we head to the hospital at once. Suddenly that car ride to the hospital triggered my contractions in such a way that the pain was coming on very strong! I mean I could barely take it! I started chanting the alphabet! I was indeed going into labor on Super Bowl Sunday!

I always envisioned being married and telling my husband, "It's time. Honey, wake up! It's time!" Then he jumps out of bed as nervous as can be to drive me quickly to the hospital. I envisioned him being with me every step of the way. That dream, that vision, never happened. I never got that moment. Yana did all she could to find out where Charles was and let him know I was in labor. Many hours have passed, and he finally arrived in the delivery room high as a kite. I had a horrific labor that went on for almost 48 hours due to all the stress of my marriage. The pain was so excruciating and unbearable I had to have a cesarean section with local anesthesia because of the hours of pressure on my body. There was no way I could bare the pain, so the option to be awake during the cesarean became not an option. My baby was born with a rapid heart rate that they were able to get down. Thank you, God! When I finally woke up, I turned my neck to the left and said my newborn's name for the first time…

Chapter 3

Jeremiah

I always knew I wanted to be a mother since I was a little girl---ever since I would take care of my dozens upon dozens of cotton stuffed animals/dolls, like my red headed cabbage patch doll, named Peggy. One day her arm ripped and out came a handful of cotton; I cried until my dad could give her the much needed one hundred plus stitches she needed. Thanks again, Dad, for saving Peggy and being her doctor. This is something I chuckle about until this day. Nevertheless, I just knew I always would be a mom, and life wouldn't be complete unless I was.

Three months after marrying Charles while he was at work, I decided I would take a pregnancy test. First, before doing so, I grabbed my black leather-bound Bible and opened it randomly.

There I placed my right hand over the chapter Jeremiah. My eyes led me to Jeremiah 1:5, "Before I formed thee in the belly, I knew thee, and before thou camest forth out of the womb, I sanctified thee, and I ordained thee a prophet unto the nations." At that moment, I felt God tap on my shoulders and tell me that I would have a boy and to name him Jeremiah. Minutes later I took the pregnancy test and started crying tears of joy! I was expecting!!! I had to surprise Charles!

That evening when Charles arrived from work, I gave him a cute little gift bag with a jar of banana baby food, my two positive pregnancy tests because one was not enough to confirm, and a card congratulating him that he was going to be a daddy! Thereafter, I proceeded to tell him that God told me we were going to have a boy and to name him Jeremiah. He instead wanted a Jr. and looked at me as if I had gone mad, insane, simply put, crazy. To be fair, it did sound a tad nuts.

A month or so had passed when Charles who worked for the United States Post Office as a mailman in the Chicago's southside neighborhood of Riverdale, Illinois, was out and about as usual on his normal route delivering packages. Suddenly, a little boy ran up to him and asked if he could help him with his mail deliveries. Charles, who was always great with kids, said, "Sure!" That cute little boy asked Charles if he had any children. He replied, "No, but my wife is having a baby." That very evening when Charles came home, he looked at me as if he had just seen a ghost. His dark tan skin as pale as it could be! Charles said, "I will never question you again."

I replied, "What do you mean?"

Charles said, "We have to name our son Jeremiah." He went on to tell me that earlier in the day that same afternoon how this little boy who was helping him on his route said to him that if we have a boy, we need to name him Jeremy, which, of course, is short for Jeremiah. Charles explained to me how at that very moment he got chills up and down his spine when that little boy said that to him. Charles knew that was confirmation of what I had told him God said to me. Our boy would be named Jeremiah.

A little over a month or so into my pregnancy, at my doctor's visit, my doctor asked me if I was taking any medication. I replied Retin-A-Topical, which is a skin cream that is sometimes used to treat molluscum. The doctor stated that he would highly recommend I get an abortion because they did a study on rats, and it revealed it can mutilate their limbs. He said the chances of my baby being born with no arms and legs would be high. I was devastated by what was said, and I left the doctor's office in tears. Walking out the door immediately looking up, I said, "God, you are the almighty physician, and I know I am supposed to have Jeremiah." On February 1st my son was born with all his fingers, toes, hands, and legs and was perfectly healthy!

To try and pour the love I have for my son onto these pages is an impossible task. Jeremiah is and will always be the love of my life---a love that is indescribable and runs deep, a love I didn't know even existed until he was born. He was the one I carried for nine months and would sing *Amazing Grace* in the shower on the top of my lungs while rubbing my belly, the one that brought me so much joy. There is no higher honor than being a mom, and I was chosen to be his mom—what a gift, and the absolute best event of my life.

I was just waking up from the anesthesia from my caesarean, and I slowly turned my head to the left to see my newborn. My baby boy was crying and in my weakened state I said, "Jeremiah". My baby stopped crying and tried to open his eyes and look at me. He recognized my voice! He knew the voice he had been hearing for the last nine months that would talk to him and sing to him was his mom. I couldn't be more in love.

Chapter 4

Extra! Extra! Read All About It!

Coming home from the hospital with our Jeremiah was indeed a new chapter. I kept staring at Jeremiah with incredible disbelief after carrying him for nine months. I mean I was looking at a miracle. This beautiful healthy boy came out of me! That being said, a huge emptiness also occurred. I had created such a bond those nine months. I found myself crying uncontrollably. When the nurse came to our home for a follow-up visit, she advised me what I was describing as experiencing the baby blues and if this kept occurring longer to advise my physician. The hardest part was the one day where no matter what I did, I couldn't stop crying. I mean ugly cry, hard cry. It was all there as I was lying face down on my bed. My husband Charles just ignored me and shouted from the living room,

"You're fine!"

Who was he to tell me what my body was feeling or the emptiness I had? Did he carry our son for nine months? Not once did he come and try to make an attempt to console me, hug me, nothing. I felt so alone. I was still in love with the fantasy of what I thought our love, our family, could be and holding on to hope. Thankfully, the baby blues didn't last past a week, and I was feeling more like myself in the coming days.

Weeks later I was trying to recuperate from my c-section, and Charles struck me again which led me to call the police. He was arrested, and I should mention it wasn't the first time I have called the police for Charles striking me. It was early March when we had our court date. My heart broke because I so badly wanted a different marriage than what we had. When the judge called us to the stand, I was holding Jeremiah in his baby seat. The judge looked at me, and she said, "Is this your child?"

I replied, "Yes, he was born last month."

The judge looked over to Charles and asked him firmly, "Did you want to have a daughter instead so you could smack her around, too?"

If I could go back in time, I would give that judge a standing ovation! However, being a young and naive twenty-two-year-old, what do you think I did? I dropped the charges!!! Again!!! Like what was I thinking? However, the state did not, and he was arrested. I had to go to Chicago's Cook County Jail and bail him out. I waited for hours upon hours until he was released in the wee hours of the morning. There was an incredibly remorseful look on his face when he came out. It was as if for the first time I could see the shame he felt for what he did. He had to know that this was unacceptable! I wasn't created to be his punching bag or anything else for that matter! He never hit me again after that. I thought we could keep what was going on in the marriage a secret. So, I thought...

I received a phone call from a good friend of mine Danica who was like family to me, an older sister if you will and Yana's cousin. I answered the call, and Danica said without hesitation, "What is going on?"

I replied, "What do you mean?"

She said, "Annie, I know. It's in the local neighborhood newspaper what Charles did to you and how he was arrested for domestic violence."

We lived in a neighborhood outside Chicago in Elmwood Park, Illinois, so I was shocked and devastated! You mean a local newspaper could plaster all my business? It was time for me not to be ashamed! I didn't do anything wrong! Why did I feel so shameful? I was so brainwashed that it is like reverse psychology that starts to shadow you until you feel so ashamed. I was so sick and tired of all the excuses! Exhausted from the new made-up stories I would tell my coworkers who have seen me come into the bank I worked at with a black eye, I had to stop accepting this lifestyle! I had to break this vicious cycle. I had to get out! How? I have a little baby and didn't make a lot of money.

I had to believe that there was a way out even when I was feeling the most helpless. How many more years was I going to put up with this manic behavior? I had stopped living and was in pure survival mode. Suddenly, survival mode became my new normal, and I was getting used to it. How sad that I was just going to accept such a lifeless life just to exist and not live? What would I be teaching my son?

Jeremiah was just a couple months shy of turning three-years-old when we separated, and I finally was brave enough to file for divorce that would officially end the marriage months later. Where did I find the courage finally to say enough is enough? I looked into my beautiful son's soulful and hopeful eyes, and I knew I needed to raise a gentleman, one who would respect his future partner and just overall be a good person to society. I have to admit there was a chunk of me that didn't want to let go of the idea of our family not being together. As you remember me saying, he did stop abusing me physically so why would I leave now? I truly love my son way too much to stay in something so unhealthy. Divorce is not easy, especially when children are involved. It isn't by no means ideal. It wasn't what I wanted when I said my vows, "I DO." However, the sound of giving my son two healthy parents individually seemed just like the right thing to do. After making that decision, I still was in a place where I didn't love me enough. The lingering mental abuse that occurred over the years was so damaging that I was starting to wonder if I would ever be cured. I felt so invisible to the world. On the outside I looked as if I had it all together. I had the bubbly laugh, big smile, an outgoing personality, and all the friends in the world, but on the inside, I was bleeding, and I felt myself dying in the mental sense. I was exhausted and couldn't understand why life had to feel so complex in my world. There had to be more to life than this.

Chapter 5

Prince Charming

Trying to accept and get comfortable with my new reality of being single again, I decided one evening after work to head over to my neighborhood gym. Cardio is not the most fun thing on my to-do list, but I got on one of the nearest treadmills, water bottle in hand ready to start feeling good about me again. I began running on the treadmill when to my surprise my future Prince Charming was also a member of the same gym! Who was this future Prince Charming you ask? Yana's friend whom I was introduced to on our girls' night out months ago. Never once did I entertain that we would ever date but just be friends. At that time, I didn't even entertain my marriage would be ending for that matter. There was an available treadmill next to me, and he jumped right on it; we started conversing. Little did I know he found out I was in the midst of a divorce and secretly had a crush on me. I, of course, was too oblivious to recognize it.

Our conversation was going great! He got off the treadmill and before walking away asked me on a date to have dinner with him. I felt a surge of butterflies and immediately said, "Yes." I have to say it was as if he was sent from God to save me from all the sadness I was feeling from my marriage ending and for a split second made me feel alive again. I felt like Cinderella in rags, and suddenly I was going to the ball! I loved the way he would look at me with the biggest grin as if I was the most beautiful woman in the world. I liked this feeling; I mean it felt good. Was I suddenly being rescued?

Saturday night had arrived! It was about a half an hour before my Prince Charming was to arrive and pick me up for our first date. I started to find myself getting flustered and reaching for the nearest bottle of wine. I started to pour myself a glass hoping to shoo the butterflies before he arrived to pick me up. Minutes later he was at my doorstep with a long-stemmed red rose in hand. He opened the passenger door for me like a true gentleman and drove us to a nice Italian restaurant that had a romantic ambiance on the northwest side of Chicago. We gazed into each other's eyes, and I could hear his heart beating, no wait---pounding with nervousness. His palms were sweaty as I appeared calm, cool, and collective. I didn't want him to know how nervous I was. Our conversations were easy and with each glass of wine more intriguing. A week had passed, and we had gone out on three dates already! We were simply crazy about each other! Our chemistry was undeniable.

Then it was my Prince Charming's birthday the following week. I planned for my Capricorn a romantic evening for two. Dinner, wine, and candles---I made sure I didn't miss a thing. His eyes told me he was captivated with every thoughtful detail. We proceeded to the living room where I told him to wait with his eyes closed. "No peeking!" I yelled. Holding with both of my hands a little round butter cream birthday cake with lighted candles on the top as I slowly made my way back from the kitchen to the living room, I started to sing, "Happy Birthday". "Make a wish!" I said. Thereafter, he read the birthday card I gave him, and everything was just wonderful. He then proceeded to rub my shoulders. That's when he leaned in brushing against my cheek, and we started to kiss, our first kiss! Finally! I thought to myself. It was the perfect first kiss! We kissed for hours, literally one, two, three hours of pure intense, intoxicating, and electrifying kissing! I felt faint. This all seemed too good to be true.

A few months had passed, and my divorce was officially final. My Prince Charming was still consistently making me feel as if I was his top priority. He wined and dined me to the best restaurants in the city always ensuring no detail was ever missed. Randomly, he would send me four dozen roses at work just because he was thinking about me. He was my definition of pure romance. One Saturday, we went to his corporate holiday party that was being held in late January. He introduced me to all his co-workers, and we ate, drank, and danced the night away. We decided to take a walk outside for a brief moment to get some fresh air. His blue eyes were gazing into mine telling me he loved me and that he has been having visions of my almost three-year-old Jeremiah being the ring bearer. I melted like butter.

There were times when I remember some days of feeling as if he was acting to be into my son for my sake. Whatever he did for my son in some instances did not feel genuine. There was a part of my gut that knew it, but there were also a lot of times he was so amazing at going to any lengths for Jeremiah as well. It was surely all in my head I thought! I was just trying to find something wrong with him, right? I mean he happily accepted that my son and I were a package deal. I wish at the time I could have realized how powerful my inner voice was being to me---if only I had trusted my intuition as if my life depended on it. Sadly, once again I would neglect it. See the truth was that in the midst of all the lavishness I did start to see several red flags. In my mind, I thought maybe I am just paranoid! Again, why was I not listening to my inner voice? The fact is I chose not to listen to it. I loved this fairytale feeling too much to let it go. I mean at times it was as if I was still that little girl who had to struggle for anything and everything she wanted. I needed this fairytale story to happen no matter what. So I chose to believe the red flags were just something I made up in my mind. Why would I sabotage this?

Meanwhile, here I am in a fairytale. Wow! I was the luckiest girl in the world! It was a year later in late December, and I was twenty-six-years-old when Prince Charming went on one knee. At that very moment, soft snowflakes started to come down gently from the sky. Light, beautiful, and magical white snowflakes! He asked me to do the honor and be his wife. I leaped in his arms and said, "YES!!!" right there on Michigan Ave. Yep! Proposal number two happened on the same street again just further down. We were at Millennium Park when he reached in his pocket holding a beautiful three-carat white gold princess cut engagement ring which now resided on my left ring finger. As we started to leave, the snowflakes suddenly stopped. Was I in some type of movie where the choreography was just right? I was living in a beautiful love story. Pinch me! My perfect Hallmark Winter Wonderland December with my Prince Charming.

About ten months later, October seventeenth, we tied the knot where Jeremiah was our handsome four-year-old ring bearer. Jeremiah would walk down with my friend Tania's beautiful three-year-old daughter who was our flower girl, Alexa. Together Jeremiah and she were just adorable! Our wedding was lavish and elegant where it could have been something out of the pages of a wedding magazine. It could be defined as spectacular! Our theme, of course, was Cinderella as I felt it was only fitting. I have to say I surely did feel like Cinderella! Everything was so perfect! Our vows were said under the gazebo with a million stars in attendance. Our guests stared at us as they listened to the sounds of love from the harpist strings; everything was just breathtaking! When we took our vows, I meant every word. I mean if I was doing this again - this was it! His eyes filled with tears as I knew this man loved me so deeply.

Then my nightmare truly began...

Chapter 6

Dark Knight

After four months of marriage, I recall us arguing yet again, and he proceeded to throw me across the laundry room. Now, to give you a clearer picture not only was he about a hundred pounds heavier than me, but he also was six-feet-five-inches towering over me. I am five feet and six and a half inches tall. He then proceeded to rip my clothes off as if he were some kind of savage. Things just kept getting worse and worse.

Roughly a month later, I was the Master of Ceremony for my college friend's wedding. My husband and I danced the night away and had a great time. Once we left and I got into the car he began to argue with me and while driving started punching me with his monstrous hands. He slammed on the brakes so fast and proceeded to throw me out of the car onto the gravel. I was in my long, beautiful gown, makeup smeared across my face and feeling as if my life was completely out of control. Luckily, there were two witnesses, that happened to be driving next to us and saw the whole thing. They quickly pulled over to see if I was okay. This sweet young couple begged me to stay with them for the evening and not go back home to where he was. The police were called, and a warrant for his arrest was made. The following Monday he turned himself in.

I was sitting in the courtroom and decided I would drop the charges. I turned to my right and there sat my two witnesses, this caring and compassionate young couple with their countenance reflecting in pure disappointment and sadness. I wish I could tell those two today how thankful I am. How courageous they were not just to be bystanders, but they took action to help a stranger. Two strangers cared more about my well-being than I had for myself.

After I dropped the charges, I felt okay. We can start over now. He now knows to take me seriously. Right? I started to think maybe he has changed. His sickness/abuse was like a volcano, always there but not sure what day it was going to erupt. I knew deep down that things would only get worse and worse! My consciousness was saying, "If you don't get out, you could risk your life. Listen, your life! Get out!" Then another evening of chaos and he pushed me so hard I almost fell out the window. I came so close to death.

How could I still be with this man? This monster? I mean he was everything a nightmare could be once we got married. Then one evening, my six-year-old son was sitting in the back seat of our car hearing his stepfather say things to me after we left a friend's party. My Dark Knight was yelling at me shouting, "Fuck you!" "You Bitch!" "You Bitch!" He was screaming at the top of his lungs while shoving his middle finger in my face. My boy Jeremiah was completely terrified. I had done everything to protect Jeremiah from witnessing something like this. I was devastated and mortified. My Dark Knight pulled over and told my son and me to get out! We were in the middle of a forest preserve. It was pitch black, and he left us there. Crying and holding my son, I was in complete shock he could do something like this. Who was this person I married?

I called Jeremiah's dad, Charles. His girlfriend who would years later become his second wife came and got us after Charles called her. She was closer to our location than where Charles was. She and I had many differences, but I will always be grateful for her being there that day. She is good to my son, and in the end all differences aside that is what matters. My ex-husband was not a good husband to me, but we were friends before and after our marriage. He had repeatedly apologized profusely for the type of husband he was to me. We knew we were way better co-parenting than being a couple, and he was and has always been in his son's life. For the record, after our divorce he truly became a wonderful father by always being present. We just weren't wonderful together.

That evening, I remember thinking I have to get out of this marriage! Then the shock that I was repeating the cycle of abuse again subsided in me. How could I let this be? What the hell was wrong with me? I have successfully up to this point in my life continued to keep the wheel spinning. I suddenly had realized I had become a nocturnal animal. My eyes had adjusted to the darkness, and now it seemed normal. With each punch, each cruel word, I was suddenly entering an ominous and toxic world and way of thinking about myself. I felt that this would be my life forever, filled with abuse. I felt so hopeless. I wasn't like the other women in their twenties, living it up and enjoying life! I was simply trying to survive.

It was the last weekend in April where my Dark Knight, another couple, and I went away for a weekend in Michigan. Saturday evening, we attended a beautiful wine dinner party at a winery in Fennville. It was such a lovely evening of laughter. My white bichon poodle named Princess came with us on this trip where she was able to have her own spa day at the Bed and Breakfast we were staying at. As the night progressed, my Dark Knight was encouraging an argument to happen. I just kept remaining positive, and he just kept egging me on trying to find something negative to complain about. He was desperately looking for a reaction. That was him, and he was relentless! I continued to act oblivious and ignore him the best I could. We then returned to our Bed and Breakfast, and my Dark Knight was falling asleep on a chair in the lobby area. I kept trying to wake him up to come upstairs to our room. How embarrassing would it be for the B&B owners to see him there and not in our room? He started to get in a rage. I mean rage! His eyes looked as if they were pitch red with anger; he then jumped up from the chair and started running after me! I ran, or shall I say flew up the stairwell as fast as I could to our bedroom so he wouldn't catch me. I felt as if I was in some horror film. I locked the door right away before he could enter. My heart was racing! He started pounding on the door to let him in! I should have dialed 911.

Chapter 7

My Nightmare

BANG! BANG! BANG! His fist pounding on the door.

"Open up the door now!" he shouted. I wanted to ensure I would

avoid a scene being made so I slowly unlocked the door. My Dark

Knight, towering me like a grizzly bear, began to beat me. His huge

hands were balled into a fist and were punching me over and over

and over again! I remember covering my face curled in a ball

waiting for him to finish. He continued to punch me harder and

harder! I was on the floor, and he took his gigantic foot and started

kicking me, my side, my back, everywhere! He then proceeded to

drag me across the bedroom floor by pulling my hair harder and

harder while asking if I liked it and if I wanted more. As he

continued to physically abuse me, he started to say hurtful and mentally abusive things, such as I was a bitch, a cunt, ugly, and I was like the "Mexicans who mowed his lawn." Those were his exact words. I felt as if my soul was being raped. Crying silently because the pain was just too much to bear, I recall my dog Princess barking and crying, but her ten-pound body could not help me against the monster that was towering over me. I thought if Princess could talk, if she could only talk. I reached for my phone to call the police, but he ripped it from my hands. When he was done with me, my dear beautiful Princess licked me and curled up with me the remainder of the night. She was my comfort and was there for me when I needed someone desperately. Thank you, my beautiful Princess. You'll never know how your love still lives on in me.

The next morning, I was in such horrific pain. There were so many knots all over my head from the punching and pulling of my hair and bruises all over my body that were black and purple. I had so much pain when I walked. Sitting down had become a task now. Still, in those moments, I thought he would feel bad and tell me he was sorry. What was wrong with me? I should have run straight for help!

Our friends were downstairs having breakfast, and my Dark Knight said to me, "Don't worry. They don't know anything that occurred last night." I put my head down and started to cry. He told me, "I got what I deserved, and no wonder my ex-husband abused me too."

Why the heck was I allowing him to make me feel as if this was my fault? It's his "make-up" to justify what he did. These are the words of a coward.

We headed down for breakfast. "May I have some orange juice please?" I ask our Bed and Breakfast host, trying not to make this breakfast any more uncomfortable and awkward than it already felt. We all sat in silence as my friends could tell something was clearly wrong. I suddenly had a surge of anger shooting through my body! I pulled my friend Lily aside and asked her to come to the bathroom with me. I pulled my pants down to show her my bruised black and purple body and what happened last night. Lily was one of my best friends, and I knew I could trust her. Her jaw dropping, filled with shock, was enough for me to know this isn't normal. That was when I had my last straw. Months prior, we had tried counseling, but any love I had for him had now turned into the purest form of disgust. It was time, and I let my Dark Knight go! I went to the courthouse and filed for an emergency divorce. I remember the day of my divorce having to go on the witness stand in front of a courtroom of strangers and answer questions about the physical and mental abuse I endured. I left that courtroom feeling free! I cried and cried some more! I was finally free! I wanted a new life! I wanted me, but who was me? That's what I had to figure out.

Chapter 8

Honey, You Got This!

I didn't want a victim mentality, but instead, I wanted to make my messes my successes---my failures, my lessons. The first few months of being alone felt fabulous. I felt a renewed energy I had never felt before! There would be the occasional feeling of loneliness when I would go to sleep at night, but overall, I had peace knowing that ending my last unhealthy marriage was the absolute right decision.

A week or so after that awful night in Michigan when I knew I had enough I spoke to a counselor over the phone explaining to her what events had taken place, I remember saying to her, "If I end this marriage, how will I look? Thirty-years-old with two divorces, surely I will be judged." Then it hit me like a ton of bricks when she replied, "So you are living your life for others, for the picture, for the show?"

Oh my gosh, yes! I was so worried about the picture and how I would be portrayed. I was willing to bear the cost of my own happiness to stay and endure it all. I knew at that moment, I wanted to be happy for me, now! I matter! My happiness matters! If there were going to be people who judge me, I wasn't going to care anymore because it was their opinion. I had to start becoming my biggest cheerleader. I started with saying to myself, "Annie, I am so proud of you! Annie, you are courageous and brave! Annie, you deserve to be happy, and from this point on, that is all that matters."

I was beyond lucky to have a supportive group around me like my family and friends, including my boss at the company I was working at who knew something was wrong. After all, we were in Human Resources, and part of our job is assessing people and relationships. I was in the midst of picking up the pieces and trying to figure out how I was going to pay for my house taxes that were soon due. My boss advised me to talk to our CEO and let him know what was going on with the abuse and the trouble I was in financially. She wanted me to see if I could possibly get a loan from the company or if there was some type of alternative option available to me. She ensured me there would be no judgement in what I had been going through the last couple of years. Our CEO/President of this very well-known company where I worked was one of the absolute kindest, humblest, and gentlest souls you could ever meet. I took the plunge and decided to tell him what was personally going on. I went into his office extremely nervous to share what was happening. I began sobbing. I proceeded to ask him if a loan would be possible to pay for my home taxes. He was so compassionate with no judgement whatsoever. He then took out his own personal checkbook, not the company checkbook, and right before my eyes wrote me a check for three thousand dollars. I promised to pay him back every cent when I would get back on my feet again. As the months went on, I went to him and said, "I am so grateful for everything you have done for me, and I am ready to start paying you back."

He looked at me and said, "Do you remember that thank you card you gave me?" Days after he gave me that check I wrote him a thank you card on how grateful I was for what he did for me and my son. I remember writing it with tears of gratitude streaming down my cheeks because of his kindness and giving heart. He proceeded to say, "Well, my wife read what I did for you in that card. She looked at me and said, "You did the right thing for her."

My CEO/President continued to say, "Listen, I just want you to be happy. I don't want you to pay me back but live a good life." I left his office with tears streaming down my face and a heart bursting with gratitude. There is no thank you that will ever do any justice to show how deeply thankful I am for people like him in this world. I know the greatest lessons he has taught me is to stay humble, be kind, and pay it forward. He is one example as is my aunt, former co-workers, friends, and many others who really helped and rallied around me in some of my darkest hours.

The next seven months I started to date a lot. I was noticing that I was still attracting men that mirrored my last two exes. I was attracting men I knew I could never have the type of future I always longed for. Nevertheless, the attention still felt great from them.

Four months later, on New Year's Day, after my divorce from the Dark Knight, I made a vow to myself I wouldn't date or be intimate with any man for at least one full year. I was committed to dating me. I knew if I wanted this vicious cycle of abuse to end, I had to get to the root of what it was about me that kept attracting these types of men in my life---the type of guy that thinks I am okay with being someone's punching bag. I knew the one common denominator my ex-husbands had in common was me. I knew stopping the cycle was going to be difficult and no easy task.

I had been in relationships since I was fifteen years old and had always gone from one relationship to the next. I actually didn't honestly realize I was never giving myself a break in between relationships until my younger sister mentioned it to me. I started to crave and develop a strong desire to get to know who I was. Who is Annie? What is my purpose? If I couldn't love myself, how could I expect someone to love me in a way I always wanted to be loved?

I yearned for a healthy relationship. I was sick of being sick! It was twenty-five plus years of not knowing what normal was, looked like, or felt like. My soul was screaming for a new life and for me to start to love myself. I knew I would have to start over by rebuilding myself and pouring a new foundation of concrete in the form of self-love.

I whisper to myself internally, "Honey, you got this!"

Chapter 9

Dating Myself

It was time to get excited about the quest of finding and loving myself! I was not oblivious to breaking a cycle that had a wheel spinning at an uncontrollable rate. I knew how the odds were stacked against me. Truthfully, I didn't care how relentless and unapologetic that wheel was. I would start with dating myself and rebuilding a new and better version of me.

Breaking a cycle meant I had to reprogram that vicious wheel. I needed to create a clear plan of action for myself which included the following for the next 12 months of my life:

- I would only date myself.

- I would not be sexually intimate with anyone. *(Yes, for at least one full year!)*

- I would be responsible for my own happiness.

- I would journal and write out all my dreams.

- I would create a vision board of the life I have always wanted.

- I would put into practice "The Law of Attraction" that I had just discovered. I would practice it to the point where it would be in my subconscious. This also meant I would flip the script with my thoughts. Whenever something negative tried to enter my mind, I would immediately say the opposite and turn it into a positive. I would feel and believe it as if it already came to fruition.

- I would write and say out-loud daily affirmations. I knew by doing this I would be rewiring and retraining my brain to think differently. Through Neuroplasticity also known as brain plasticity, I would rewire my brains thoughts. Without a doubt I needed a new mindset.

I truly wanted to start over and have the life I knew I

deserved, but I had to do a couple of other things first. I needed to get comfortable with being alone.

Challenge number one was to go to the movies by myself. Yes, take myself out on a date on one of the coldest January evenings. My former thinking was that movies were meant to be an activity with friends or where you would go on a date. Nonetheless, I wanted to start with this activity and see a romantic film, being the hopeless romantic that I am. It's also one of my favorite genres to watch besides comedies. So why not? I chose to see the film *P.S. I Love You*. I wasn't forewarned, but gosh it's a tear-jerker! I grabbed my coat excited about the date with myself and drove to the cinema! "Ticket for one please," I stated to the guy in the booth. I proceeded to the concession stand and purchased a big bucket of salty buttery popcorn. I started to walk my way towards the back of the theater and find my comfy seat. Sitting there in the back, I realized that the cinema was filled with couples, and I couldn't help but feel so proud of myself for doing this for me. The movie ended, and I had an epiphany!

I realized at least for me that divorce is truly like a death.

Granted there was no divorce in the movie, but there was a loss.

Once the movie finished, I drove to a secluded spot and allowed myself to weep, and I mean uncontrollably weep, ugly cry and all! I allowed myself to mourn the death of my marriage. I had seemed fine for so many months thereafter. It was as if I was numbing the pain without realizing I was. While I was in my parked secluded spot, I decided I would bury the pain and anger for what my Dark Knight did to me in exchange for inner peace. I said out loud, "Annie, it's okay to hurt. It's okay to be sad things didn't work." I whispered to myself, "Now let go. Let go. Let the anger go. Let the dreams go. Let it all go. Let him go." I knew I wasn't going to look back anymore. There was no future in the past.

I slowly got out of my car and went to a grassy area where some of the snow had already melted away. Inside my purse, I had a wallet sized wedding picture of the Dark Knight and me and a diamond heart pendant he had given to me when we were together. I was still carrying these two items with me for the last seven months. I decided right there and then I was going to have a funeral. I would bury his heart and our marriage. It was time for me to officially say goodbye for the last time. Once I buried the photo and diamond heart pendant, I suddenly felt a huge shift occurring. The shift I was feeling was filled with empowerment! Enlightenment had presented itself to me for the first time. Tears flowed down my cheeks as I got back in my car to drive home. It was like watching a cluster of clouds covered in darkness suddenly allowing the sun to seep through. Even the breeze and each breath I took seemed different. I started to smile bigger and bigger with each passing traffic light. It was as if the real Annie had peaked out for the first time with joy because there were no bars holding me back. This was the beginning of my healing.

Since I was eleven years old, travel was always my love language. I had only been to three countries at this point but never Europe. The last five years, my desire to see and explore Europe grew exponentially! My wanderlust spirit saying repeatedly, "When do we leave?" One evening while working late, I took a break and decided to search the internet typing: *European vacation.* Suddenly, fate stepped in, and there was a tour that seemed like the perfect fit. Based on the reviews, it seemed as if it would be a ton of fun! They had several tour packages, and it was geared for ages eighteen to thirty-five-year-olds. I thought why not call the travel agent and get more details? I knew I didn't have the money, but I had been doing my affirmations and practicing The Law of Attraction religiously. I began saying to myself, "I can't wait to see Europe!" I believed it, felt it, and envisioned myself there. I started taking action by googling the possibilities. I took action by creating a vision board that was filled with Europe plastered all over it!

The trip was well over a thousand dollars excluding the international flight. I mean I was lucky if I had any extra money lingering in my bank account after my paycheck. The agent stated I needed two hundred dollars to pay today to secure my spot, and the rest would be due months later. I knew I was ready to create new experiences! I only saw this as another opportunity for me to continue dating myself some more. I decided to listen to my inner voice shouting, "DO IT!" and I did!!! It was the end of January when I officially booked my two-week trip to seven European countries *(United Kingdom, Netherlands, Germany, Austria, Switzerland, Italy, and France),* scheduled to leave the end of June and going into the beginning of July. Approximately five months away!!!! I could barely contain my excitement! This would be my first time traveling completely solo besides the time I flew to Honduras by myself when I was thirteen years old to see my dad's side of the family. My first European adventure was awaiting me! I would be turning thirty-two-years-old on July second while traveling on this adventure. What an amazing birthday gift I was giving to myself! I loved that I honestly booked it without knowing how I would be able to pay the remaining balance of the trip. I wasn't even sure if my employer would approve all this time off. What I did know was that I was going to go and trust that God/universe had my back! I knew this is what my soul needed.

It was the month of June when I brought to my office my red Diane von Furstenberg suitcase that I saved up for and bought on eBay. I was packed and ready to go at the end of the workday. It was so hard to concentrate at work because I was filled with excitement and a ton of gratitude. God/universe was working in my favor the whole time. I just had to act! I mean the Bible even says, "Ask and you shall receive". That's exactly what happened! I received an unexpected bonus months prior which paid for the remaining balance of my trip, and my time off from my employer was approved. The Law of Attraction was starting to show me I did have the power to manifest the things and experiences I have always dreamed of!

I arrived at the airport, and I began to journal all my deepest thoughts that I was feeling before boarding to my first destination London, England. Let's just say that trip not only gave me a love affair of Europe but created an even deeper wanderlust. The lifelong friends made, the different cultures, the crazy stories, and so much more will forever be embedded in my mind. I was blessed to have had the most fun and most knowledgeable tour guide to lead our group of eighteen to thirty-five-year-olds Kerri from South Africa! I am always grateful she never let the bus leave me all the times I came back late and oh, that one time everyone thought I went missing in St. Goar, Germany, when they realized I hadn't been in my room all night because I was locked out accidentally. I hung out part of the night gazing at the stars on the Rhine River with two local Germans. To my right was a guy who truly mirrored Andre the Giant and to my left sat an attractive German guy who was really hoping I would ditch this tour and jump on his motorcycle to accompany him to Munich. The stories were endless on this trip! This truly set my heart off to a road filled with wanderlust. The possibilities started to seem endless!

I began to realize I was the one holding me back from all these incredible experiences prior to dating myself. I used to think small, dream small, but now I was beginning to think bigger! My dreams were possible no matter how big or crazy they may seem!

My dating myself quest didn't end there, of course. Other things I did to date myself would be evenings filled with soft music such as jazz or Irish songs because the lyrics and instruments just made me feel happy. I wanted to keep my vibrations on a high feel-good frequency. I would light candles that emitted soft romantic lights, and I would drink a glass of some red, lush, velvety wine as I relaxed on my plush sofa being so grateful for the peace and happiness I was feeling. I would buy myself bright flowers or a dozen long-stemmed roses and write on the card, "I love you, Annie." I would continue to say to myself, "You deserve this,

Annie." I would practice saying kind words to myself even if I didn't believe it. Years of mental abuse meant reprogramming my mind daily. Did it feel ridiculous at times? Yes, in the beginning it did, but the more I did it the more I believed I deserved it. This is how I was creating new energy and rewiring my thoughts. Dating myself gave me a newfound confidence. I was no longer dependent on a man or anyone for that matter to make me happy. I learned my happiness had to come from within. Wow! What a revelation! I had the key to my happiness the whole time, and all I had to do was turn the key!

Time after time I had this notion that something or someone else was what I needed to feel fulfilled. I missed out on looking inward to examine the many beautiful layers I already had within. Dating myself for one whole year and sticking with that commitment served me well in a million ways. The commitment I made said in exclamation points, "I AM WORTH IT!"

Chapter 10

The Whole Pie

Often in relationships, we make exceptions and/or excuses whether to start or not to start dating someone. I have done this many of times. Some of us have high standards while others perhaps do not have enough. Some of us are focusing way too much on the shallow aspects whereas that is usually an excuse to distract us from what is important in a partner.

Something interesting I found very common in my numerous conversations I have had with many friends including myself was that there was a common theme when it came to choosing and making exceptions for the wrong partner(s). It goes something like this: "He/She is great BUT!" "He/She treats me well BUT!" "He/She spoils me with gifts BUT!" "He/She only hits me once in a while BUT." "He/She is the father/mother of my child BUT." "He/She only cheated on me once BUT." or "He/She works hard BUT." "He/She loves me BUT." and so on and so on! The list goes on and on. We make tons of excuses! I know I have made excuses and exceptions because I wanted so badly to believe they would change. The truth of the matter was the fact I was simply in love with the fantasy of the potential I thought they could be in the relationship. I was continuing to make excuses as to why the eighth slice of pie was missing in my past partners. I was consistently accepting partial pies.

Let me explain. Let's say you were at a bakery that was selling a wide array of pies. You choose an apple pie and proceed to the counter to pay for it. You suddenly realize there are only seven slices and not your typical eight pie slices that you would get when you purchase a whole pie. Would you still pay full price for that pie? Seven slices for the price of eight? No way! It wouldn't make any sense for even the cashier to justify it. You would think at the very least a discount should apply. So why in our own lives do we accept partial pie? A discounted version? Do we not think we deserve the whole pie? Of course, we deserve the whole damn pie! All eight slices! If the universe knows you are willing to have half a pie, quarter of a pie, then guess what? You will continue to get what you accept. You will continue to get what you say you don't want. Your words and thoughts are powerful. Choose what you want and take action by speaking it into existence rather than telling everyone else including yourself that you will never find the right partner. The universe will grant you just that. Instead say, "I am open and willing to receive love, and I am so excited I am meeting my partner." Think, feel, and believe as if it already has happened.

It can be mind-boggling and such a shame that we actually pay more attention to the complete pie we would buy at a bakery than to the lacking qualities/characteristics of our partner in our own life. We have to stop making excuses as to why the eighth slice of pie is missing in our partner. It's about cutting the fat on all the excuses we make on why we should or shouldn't stay in that relationship, friendship, and or job.

This pie method has allowed me and others I have shared this with to get clear as well as narrow down what we truly envision is important in a partner. It's time we stop willingly taking the discounted version of who we choose as our life partner. After having made a ton of mistakes in my twenties with picking the wrong guys, it was crucial for me to come up with a formula to really get clear of what I wanted. I was very clear of what I didn't want. When I started to think about what my slices were, I first wrote down everything I wanted in a partner from looks to traits and so on. I had well over one hundred things written down! It wasn't hard to do as I made sure to capture every detail. Then after combing through each of those one hundred plus bullet points, I chose the eight that were the most important to me. This also took out all the shallow excuses I would give myself as to why I would not go on a date with someone who perhaps wasn't my type. It made me get really intentional about what exactly I was looking for. This process allows us to zoom in and focus. Now, I want to preface first by saying that on top of the eight slices before anything you need to feel a connection. I don't mean chemistry. We often get so confused between connection and chemistry. If you have a connection, the chemistry can come. The connection is the meeting of two inner souls. You can't understand it, and it can't be forced. That is one of the beauties of that initial encounter being present and tuned in to that connection. It's a beautiful thing! How many times have you heard people's story on how they met their partner, but at first, they didn't think they were their type just by looking at a picture? Maybe they could never imagine someone like him/her could be his/her person, his/her partner. However, after conversations, laughing, getting to know who this person is, a connection is felt. Something like a light switch turns on, and the way you look at him/her simply shifts!

Once we have established the connection, that is when you should refer to your pie chart that you have written out. To view the "pie theory" think of a whole pie with eight slices. Let's say each slice represents a quality that you would say is a must for a successful relationship. For example, pie slice number one could be: *RESPECT*. Pie slice number two could be: *LOYALTY*. Pie slice number three could be: *SENSE OF HUMOR*. Pie slice number four could be: *LOVE*. Pie slice number five could be: *HONESTY*. Pie slice number six could be: *COMMUNICATES WELL*. Pie slice number seven could be: *SPONTANEOUS*. Pie slice number eight could be: *A HARD WORKER*. Hey, if being tall is a MUST, write:

TALL. The beauty of pies is that it comes in different flavors, and everyone has a different palate so to speak. My pie slices may be different than yours, and that is A-Okay! These are just a few slices to give you an idea. Once a connection is made, and one of the slices/traits is missing in them, well guess what? You are cheating yourself and in my opinion are indeed settling. This just helps the dating process and with so many of us wasting our time!

When I personally started to narrow my list, or should I say my detailed scroll down from over one hundred to eight traits, it truly gave me perspective to what is important in a partner of my dreams. I am going to share my personal 8 slices of pie that I want in a partner in no particular order. It's also not to say that in ten or twenty years my pie slices could change. We evolve and grow as people! However, I could take control of present me.

For me, I don't know if I will ever remarry, or if I would divorce again. I just know from this point forward, I will always choose me first.

Annie's 8 pie slices:

#1 <u>Sense of Humor</u> - Someone who loves to laugh as much as he loves to breathe. A sense of humor is extremely sexy to me!

#2 <u>Romantic</u> - What can I say? I am the true definition of a hopeless romantic! I know for me it is an essential ingredient. The cheesier the better for me! Yes, I know a lot of you will probably want to barf or skip this as your slice, but hey this is my pie slice!

#3 <u>Adventurous</u> - An adventurous person who tells me he is passionate about life. He has a spontaneous spirit that would want to seek and live life to the fullest. We push each other out of our comfort zones to create the ultimate experiences.

#4 <u>Loyal</u> - My partner is loyal---period---loyal in all relationships whether it be with me, family, or friends. A loyal partner is one who doesn't need outside validation. He is confident and wants to share a truly profound love with his partner - me.

#5 <u>Intimate/Affectionate</u> - My love language is touch so I know it is vital for me to have this quality in a partner. I want my partner's hands all over me! Daily kisses, cuddling, intimacy, yes please!

#6 <u>No Bad Habits</u> - This pie slice means no addictions, such as smoking, drugs, anger, negativity, etc. I have realized from my past relationships I can't save anyone who doesn't want to save himself. I am looking to now have the opposite which is a partner who is a hundred percent whole.

#7 <u>Positive/Respectful about Life, My Son and Me</u> - A partner who has a zest for life and can appreciate my free spirit! He treats me the way I deserve to be treated. When I catch him glimpsing over at me, his eyes say, "Wow, I'm the luckiest guy on the planet." He is someone who knows my son and I are a package deal and sees that not only as a blessing but also as an honor to be in both of our lives!

#8 <u>Financially Secure</u> - What I mean by this is that a partner who can take care of himself. I want to know he can carry his weight and support himself financially.

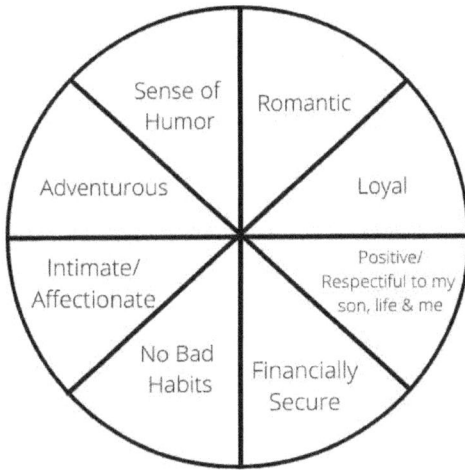

Yes, of course, you can write down even more traits. However, your CORE eight slices should serve as a guide to give you clarity not to compromise any of those traits once a connection is made. As I mentioned before when I did this exercise, I wrote down over a hundred traits, but my eight were non-negotiable.

Here is a great opportunity to truly think about every single handful of traits or one hundred plus traits, characteristics, description that you are looking for in a partner. Get as detailed as possible! Jot them down:

_____

_____

_____

_____

_____

_____

_____

Now take a look at what you wrote and select from the list your eight most important and non-negotiable pie slices aka traits that once a connection is made you refer to this for clarity.

My eight non-negotiable romantic relationship pie slices:

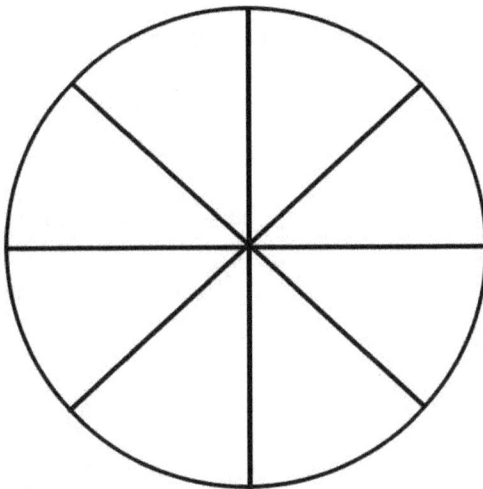

Let's expand the pie theory even further. What about your friendships? Your environment in all forms is equivalently just as important. You need to be conscientious of who you allow in your circle and in your life. Think about the five people you hang around with the most. If your circle is very small, then think about who do you listen to the most? An example can be podcasts. Maybe you spend hours on the road, and this is who you let in your headspace day in and day out. Be conscientious of that because what you feed the mind you will attract.

When you think about your circle of friends or your best friend, do they have your eight core slices/traits that you would want to be around? Do you feel energized after a conversation with them, or do you leave them feeling drained? Do they inspire you, or do they not inspire you? Do you feel empowered or not empowered?

Below is another pie chart for you to write down the eight "slices" of who you want in your circle of friends/your tribe to have.

My eight non-negotiable friendship pie slices are:

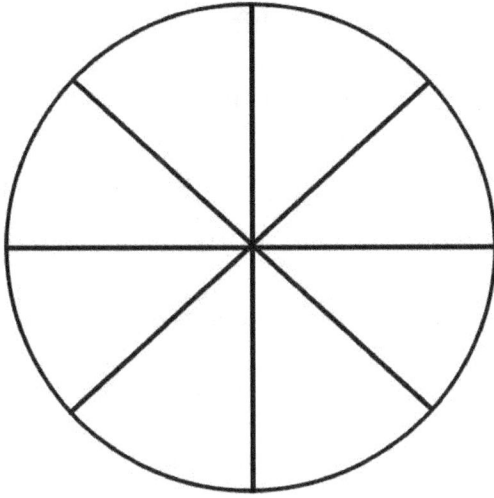

We talked about romantic relationships and friendships but what about your work environment? For many of us we spend time with our coworkers and bosses more than our own families. This is very important!

An example is when I was in my mid-thirties, I knew that if I was going to go back into corporate America that I was going to get very clear of what it must have. I knew I wasn't going to settle just to get a paycheck. I began writing everything I wanted down. I closed my eyes and envisioned what I wanted, what it would look like and feel like, and more! I wrote a list out very similar to the list I wrote out that I wanted for my romantic relationships. I went as far as how I wanted the office to look like with plants, how good I would feel coming in, the work life balance, etc. Guess what? I got a call and left that interview knowing this was going to be my new employment! I mean it was everything I was looking for, and my intuition was shouting, "This is it! This is it!" I am grateful for that list because I truly did make some amazing memories and created lifelong friendships. It was a job that allowed my wanderlust and free spirit to soar! I got so intentional on the type of freedom and flexibility I wanted before being offered that position. I was even able to travel to seven continents in one year while still being able to perform my 9-5 job. It didn't happen accidentally; it happened because I was intentional of what I wanted and envisioned it.

I know I sound like a broken record, but it is very important to get intentional. I mean *really* intentional. If I gave you a magic wand and you could create exactly what you wanted in your work setting, what would it be? What would it feel like?

Here is another opportunity to write them down.

My eight non-negotiable workspace/coworker(s) relationship pie slices:

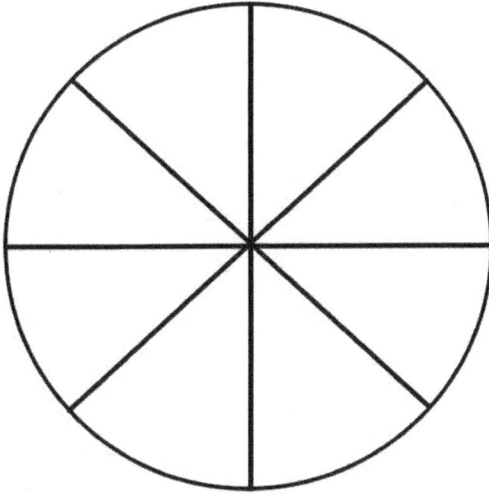

When you look at your pie charts whether it be romantic relationships, friendships, and the workplace, you now have a clear road map. If you aren't exactly sure, then write down the things that you don't want. Then the opposite would be applicable to what it is that you do want. The more and more you think about it, the more you will attract the very thing, person, and situation you want in your life. I am proof that The Law of Attraction consistently gives attention to where your focus goes.

Chapter 11

The Goodie Bag

I started to ponder about my mini hiatus from intimacy. I wasn't the person who judged others on their personal decisions when it came to sleeping around with what some may say as too soon. I mean as long as they were responsible and safe, that was the most important in my mind. Who was I to judge? However, what I didn't understand was how shocked some of my friends were when they expected a long-lasting relationship after just having a night of intimate pleasure without their interest not working for it.

I started to remember when I was a child how I would go to my friends' birthday parties growing up and how I would always look forward to the very end! You know the part when one of the parents would hand out a goodie bag filled with different fun filled items like toys, candy, etc. as a thank you for coming. Nobody would dare imagine entering the party at the beginning and say, "I want my goodie bag now please." No, you had to wait until the end of the party to receive it.

Listen, some of you are wondering why when you start dating someone, he isn't taking you seriously. Let me ask you this. Are you handing out your "goodie bag" before the party even begins? Now, I personally don't think that giving out your goodie bag early is wrong IF you are clear to whom you are with that your only intention is to give and get a goodie bag. I mean more power to you! I get it. We all have needs. However, if you think you can just sleep with someone with expectations of something more, you may want to rethink that. Years ago, there was a movie made called *Vanilla Sky* that starred Tom Cruise who played David Aames and Cameron Diaz who played Julianna (Julie) Gianni. David thinks Julie is fine with their casual sexual relationship. To be fair I think Julie thinks she is fine with it, too. As time goes on, David begins to date Penelope Cruz's character named Sofia, and now Julie isn't happy. There is a scene---a scene that truly stuck with me. Julie is in the car with David, and she says, "Don't you know that when you sleep with someone, your body makes a promise whether you do or not?" Especially with ladies, the chemical our bodies produce after sex is called oxytocin, also known as the "cuddle hormone" which is known to affect our behavior.

I have a very close friend, one of my circle of best friends who was basically Julie from *Vanilla Sky*. She truly thought and was a hundred percent convinced that she would never develop any feelings for her "David". It would be strictly just a physical exchange and enjoying the entanglement of their two bodies. As months went on, she started to fall for him hard and unexpectedly.

So, if you are the one who is truly looking for something serious, then I say take your time and stay for a while at the party. Date and get to know each other first. Emphasize the value of your goody bag. Enjoy his/her company; take your time to get to know the person. Don't think your goody bag is the ticket to commitment. Ultimately, you will be the one they will desire more. Have a goodie bag that is hard to get. Become that party that is hard to get the invite to.

I knew that after I got to my one year of no sexual encounters, that I would want to still wait until I found that special someone for me. I wanted to have the most desired goodie bag for my future someone!

Chapter 12

A Guarantee Please!

Aren't we all afraid of the unknown? It's often when we are at the brink of an amazing life changing discovery, we take two steps back rather than leaping in with both feet forward! So many times, we are so close to our dreams, but when we feel it isn't working the way we think it should, we suddenly give up. What a shame when you were so close! Why do we put one foot on the side of chance and the other feet planted on the safety net?

I have learned to use that feeling of fear as a signal indicator to GO FOR IT! When I say fear, I am strictly talking about the fear of taking risks on our dreams or that gut feeling, intuition that you know you were meant for something more. I mean fear is an invitation with open arms to take a step closer to who you were meant to be on this planet. One of the scariest things for me that I have feared was being so vulnerable to strangers and even to my friends, fear of how they would judge me. I know now that being able to let go and do so is the gift. It took me a long time to realize that that feeling of fear, my gut pulling intuition voice had been a blessing in disguise. I just was ignoring it or thinking the signal of fear was there to talk me out of it. It's those thoughts that kept me from living on purpose for so long. I finally chose not to be a prisoner to my fears. I chose my fear to be my ally, a built-in detector saying, "Everything you want is on the other side of fear." Thank you, Jack Canfield, for that amazing quote by the way! Growth started to come when I decided to start pushing through that fear so that I could ultimately reach each of my goals and dreams. I encourage you to do the same!

It is our innate human nature to want a guarantee before we place all our eggs in one basket and take that risk. I had defined failure as it's over or it wasn't meant to be and so on. I didn't equate the failures as lessons and as stepping-stones that were leading me to the path and road to success. I knew I was not going to reap rewards with having a guarantee. Besides, where is the fun in that? That is what makes the success when it comes so rewarding because of taking those scary risks and actions when there were no guarantees.

This is another way also to know if you are alignment with the universe. Focus and take action toward the life you want and know that the universe must respond to your vibration.

If you are willing to take a chance on yourself, and if you are willing to take a risk without any guarantees, then you will see the doors of the universe opening for you. It's normal to be afraid, and when your heart starts to race, what that means to me personally is that something amazing is about to happen! That is when I just keep walking forward and not allow my fears to talk me out of it. I knew I was worthy of having a rich and fulfilling life that has more than I could ever imagine all because I took a chance, a chance on someone worth it - ME!

Chapter 13

Thank You, Today Show

One morning I found myself flipping through television show after television show before heading out to work, and for some reason when it landed on the *Today Show*, a popular morning show in the United States, a whisper said, "Record it." I didn't understand it, but nevertheless, I pressed record, and off to work I went. Later that evening, I decided to watch that morning's program of the *Today Show* I had recorded, and there was a segment on how inexpensive it was to travel to Barcelona, Spain, the capital of Catalunya. I thought to myself, Holy Moly! What a steal! Approximately six hundred U.S. dollars to fly to Barcelona with the hotel included for almost a week! Several days later my friend Lily came over, and I had to share that segment of the show with her. She was so blown away too that she canceled her planned trip to Hawaii with her husband John, so we all could head to Barcelona together for her birthday week in March. Another country under my belt? Yes, please!

A few months prior before this trip would ever come to fruition, I was sitting in my office on a cold December day at work, and my mind started to drift. I started to feel a strong wanderlust sensation implode all over me. Deep in the pit of my soul craved a desire to obtain a more zealous and freeing life that included seeing the world with a broader lens. Then my mind began to race relentlessly repeating deep in the crevices of my brain like a broken record:

"There has to be more to life than just this, me sitting behind a desk."

My mind kept constantly dreaming about going to another country to explore and learn all I could about its culture. I was just starting to practice religiously The Law of Attraction learning to condition my thoughts. I knew that my thoughts were where all my dreams, ideas, and visions started from. Every one of my thoughts represented a seed that could start to blossom into a life I had always envisioned. I was training my mind to start to visualize the most audacious dreams ever! Travel was one of the things I always dreamt of being able to do frequently. I received one vicious bite of the Travel Bug at age eleven when I jumped up and down like a kid in a candy store when I had an opportunity to cross the border for the day from Illinois to Indiana. Indiana? Who gets excited to travel to Indiana? I did! I just wanted to travel, and I didn't care where! There I was in a deep daydream pondering the thought of how awesome it would be to be in Spain and learn Spanish. After all I am half Spanish, and it is my dad's native tongue. He just never taught us it growing-up since he and my mother thought it would confuse us three kids. I have always been fascinated by languages, and to learn Spanish would be a dream come true! My thoughts kept swirling deeper and deeper. Hmmm, why not move and teach English in Madrid for income? I started to google information on how it would be possible to teach English as a second language. I even called schools to gather information on what requirements I needed to do so. I continued talking to my drifting mind convincing my subconscious that it might be possible to do for a summer so my son's school year would not be interrupted. I searched for apartments in Madrid, and my mind began to envision all the endless possibilities. One day perhaps, one day.

So here I was three months later at O'Hare International Airport about to finally board with Lily and John to Barcelona for five full days. I was not just flying to Barcelona, but I was flying high on the adrenaline of life! I loved how happy I had finally become and how much I was not just loving life but living life! I had felt a predominant shift of newly found energy after having done so much work on loving myself and dating me the past fifteen months. Contentment, gratitude, and peace flooded every fiber within the depths of my soul.

Exploring beautiful and vibrant Barcelona for the first time was like landing in a city that had every ingredient one could ask for---the art, history, architecture, beaches, the Catalan people, language and culture, and the food which included savory tapas! Oh, and let's not forget the variety of Spanish wines and sparkling crisp Cava that could taunt anyone's palette! I was in a magical city soaking it all up.

A couple days later it was Lily's birthday! I got up early and swiftly headed down the corridor to Lily and John's hotel room. Knock! Knock! The door opened, and my extroverted self began to sing at the top of my lungs Happy Birthday! It was time to get this celebration started! That evening the three of us headed to an elegant restaurant that was recommended by a colleague. This place perfected what it meant to give the guest an incredible experience with top notch hospitality. Our waiter began to display multiple dishes of all the yummy choices we could have for dinner. "Here we have the irresistible lamb eyes and over here is a dish of our succulent prawns." It was as if the prawn's long antennas raised up while staring down at us with their black beady eyes. I could feel the energy of the three of us slowly going into a deep state of shock. Gulp! I internally tried not to gag as it's hard enough for me to eat any meat that has any sort of bone or that looks like an animal. It definitely made for an interesting start to the evening. Thank goodness a yummy and sizzling filet mignon was an option for dinner. Spanish red wine kept pouring, and oh, how luscious it was!

Pairing it with a plump and juicy chocolate covered strawberry was heavenly. I mean the two blends were the perfect marriage, just meant to be together if you will. We ended the dinner with a photo with our main waiter who honestly resembled Phil Collins. When I told him that, he chuckled and proceeded to sing a chord from one of Phil Collins songs: Sussudio! It was a great way to end dinner. What I didn't know was how my life was about to change later that evening.

Chapter 14

The Unexpected

Lily, one of my best friends, and John, Lily's husband, was like a big brother to me; we enjoyed traveling together. I never felt like the third wheel ever. Four and a half months prior to our Barcelona excursion, the three of us traveled together to Ireland for the weekend. Yes, just for a weekend living our best life! We really loved Irish pubs and all the good energy it always seemed to bring. It also seemed as if it attracted a fun crowd. So, of course, it only made sense that we all decided to go to an Irish Pub located in Las Ramblas which is a very touristy and famous part of Barcelona. We started with some perfectly poured pints of Guinness sitting at the bar toasting to Lily's birthday. Thereafter, it was time to have a celebratory birthday shot of baby Guinness! I was just having a blast in this old world crowded Irish pub, laughing loudly and loving life!

There in the back of the pub stood a man who would be admiring me from a distance and work his way through the crowd to find his way towards me.

He approached me with a strong gaze, and when my eyes locked his, I was intoxicated, and I don't mean because of the drinks. If there was truly a thing called love at first sight or as the French call it "Le coupe de foudre", this was it! Suddenly the earth stood still, and everyone around me just froze. I was in a sudden trance as our eyes continued to lock almost as if we were looking into each other's soul. He leaned in closer to me, and his lips started gravitating towards mine slowly; he began to press passionately against them---so soft and subtle yet strong and forceful that the kiss couldn't be stopped even if we tried. It was like invisible fireworks over us! Lily and John were in a sudden shock as they looked to their right to witness their friend in a heated exchange. I knew before, during, and after that kiss, we both felt something so strong like an electric current that would not let go and continue to pull you in. We couldn't ignore it and didn't even try to fight it just surrendering willingly. I knew there was something so different about him. He wasn't like any other man I had been with before, and what I mean by that was his energy, his look, HIM...... it was all new and different but a good difference, an exciting difference.

The four of us left the Irish pub in Las Ramblas to continue celebrating Lily's birthday when suddenly out of the blue John's camera was stolen. This definitely put a damper on their evening, and they were ready to call it a night. However, I knew I didn't want my night to end. I wanted the evening to quite frankly never end. I wanted to continue the night with my French lover named Lucas as much as he did. He was from Paris but also Basque Country in a part of France in a city called Bayonne. So, I did something I have never done and asked him if he wanted to come back to my hotel and just talk and kiss some more and perhaps have a glass of Spanish red wine that I purchased earlier in the day. I continued to keep in mind that I had not had any sexual relations/sex in any form for the last fifteen months at this point. I was dating myself and working on shifting the type of men I was attracting in my life. I also mentally reminded myself that under no circumstances---no matter how hard it could be---that I would not have sexual intercourse tonight. I had committed to myself that the next time I would be intimate it would be because it was with the right person, someone I was in love with and in a committed relationship with. I can't explain what I felt, but I knew he felt safe, and something just felt right. My intuition made a strong statement that gave me the clearance I needed to say that this was going to turn out fine. After I asked Lucas to come back with me, he excitedly exclaimed, "YES! I would love to and spend more time with you!".

We arrived at my hotel the U232, and as soon as we got to my room, we opened that bottle of red wine and talked for hours upon hours in Spanish. His first language was French, and his English was average. My Spanish at the time was not good at all. I knew basic survival Spanish, but somehow, we made it work like a game of charades. Was this how my parents communicated when they met so many years ago when they didn't speak the same language? Lucas and I were definitely communicating the language of love as we passionately kissed each other for hours as we found our way to my bed. We continued to discover our bodies, feeling nothing but pure passion as our naked bodies pressed against each other. Lucas literally kissed every centimeter of my body not missing a thing. I mean he made my knee feel just as important as my elbow or breast. I was his masterpiece he was exploring slowly and delicately with the tip of his tongue. He was gentle and warm and, my God, so full of explosive passion! My body was yearning for him as silent moans vibrated off the hotel walls just from his touch. I was exploding with passion and wanted so badly to make love to him, but I couldn't because I made a commitment to myself, I was keeping no matter what the circumstance. I had to honor that, and when I said no, he respected my no in true gentleman form and pleasing me suddenly became his mission that evening or shall I say early in the wee hours of the morning. All my "delicates" sang from the rooftop as his mission was more than just complete. Lucas made me feel as if I was floating in ecstasy.

Early that morning he asked me if I would like to have breakfast with him. He also made mention that he didn't want to interfere with my trip with my friends either. He looked at me with his dark brown eyes and wispy, silk black hair that rested perfectly against his face saying, "I would love to see you again."

"Here is my phone number," he replied.

"Okay, I will call you later and let you know," I stated.

He left my room as I didn't have time to have breakfast with him that morning. I went down to the lobby deliriously feeling as if my heart was going to race out of my chest from Lucas's lingering touch. Lily and John were waiting for me there while asking the concierge to make our dinner reservations for our last evening in Barcelona. In the midst of the concierge on the phone making our dinner reservations for three, I said out loud, "Make it four!" A sudden grin, a smirk from Lily and John's faces, arose. They both really liked him, too, so I called my French lover and said to him to come to dinner with us. My friends and I just had a long day exploring the beautiful city of Barcelona and all that the brilliant Gaudi had to offer. We headed back to the hotel so that we could shower and get ready for dinner. We entered our hotel lobby, and there sat Lucas waiting for me. "Give me about twenty minutes to get ready." I said excitedly. Racing to my room to get ready as quickly as possible he continued to wait patiently in the lobby. Lucas was occupying his time with his brilliant brain of mathematics. He had a PHD in mathematics and was a pure mathematician genius. He spoke seven languages, and, gosh, his personality was larger than life, his laugh so infectious, and his accent made me melt like butter! He was fun and intense and had so many ingredients I had been looking for!

We all headed out to the El Canejo Loco, a swanky restaurant in Barcelona overlooking the sea in Port Olympic. The ambience couldn't be more perfect for a first official date, or should I say double date. The conversation was flowing, and we laughed so much. He began singing some Metallica, and we were loving his energy! I really was falling hard for this guy! I could listen to Lucas's French accent all day. I admired his quirkiness from afar and loved his zest for life! Sitting across from Lily and John, Lucas would grab my hand and start kissing it until his soft lips reached all the way to the top of my shoulder like the cartoon character, the skunk Pepé Le Pew. He didn't care that my friends were sitting across from us. He was so comfortable with who he was and didn't care who or where or how he expressed what he felt. Gosh, it was so sexy! He was the epitome of the whole package. It's just what my gut was feeling. I thought to myself just to enjoy the evening with him, my vacation fling. As hours passed, I asked Lily to go to the bathroom with me as I couldn't wait to express to her how much I liked this guy. I mean really liked him. She concurred and agreed saying, "He is a pretty amazing guy!"

After dinner we headed down the strip in Port Olympic and began drinking, dancing, chatting, and just having a blast as to what would be our last evening in Barcelona before catching our flight to Chicago the next day. I couldn't bear thinking this would be my last evening with Lucas. We all headed back to the hotel in the wee hours of the morning an hour before we had to actually pack and leave! We used that last hour to caress each other and hold onto each other tightly. His touch was so soft and gentle that he made my body quiver and shiver! Lucas continued to respect my wishes of no sexual intercourse with ONE no and instead took my body as a delicate rose exploring every inch and placing me back in the land of ecstasy for a second time!

That morning as we stood in front of the hotel, there was our cab awaiting to transport Lily, John, and me back to the airport. My friends proceeded to get into the taxicab, and Lucas and I started to have one last strong and passionate kiss. We continued with a strong embrace never wanting to let go. However, it was time for me to say goodbye, goodbye forever. Then he looked at me in the eyes and before entering the cab his last words to me were, "I love you." I can't deny the feeling that I felt when he said those three words to me. It was a shock that he said I love you just after a couple of days together. Lucas was a very passionate man, and we truly experienced love at first sight in every way. I was in the cab now with warm sensations all over me feeling such a deep sadness that that would be the last time I would ever see him again.

Chapter 15

Take the Leap!

I was back in the United States, and I literally knew I was going to move to Barcelona. I remembered months earlier about my prior thoughts of doing so but in Madrid. My French lover Lucas was not the sole reason at all for moving, but it definitely was the push I needed to pull the trigger. I am a single mom with a beautiful son, have a great job, have the house, and all, so the question to many would be why on earth would I want to leave all this stability? I always personally felt there was more to life than the "American Dream" everyone keeps continuously painting which just didn't seem right for me.

You have to start to appreciate that life does open doors and that the universe will flood your life with blessings if you just believe. Don't worry about how it will happen, just know, and let the universe/God do the how. It's your constant actions that will throw the right scenario in your path. The how isn't your business in my opinion, but it is the number one reason people stop dreaming big because they focus way too much on how it could possibly happen for them.

That following Saturday afternoon after coming back from my trip to Barcelona, I headed to my friend's house Danica, my adopted big sister. I mentioned how I felt I should go and move to Spain but was worried how it would be for my son Jeremiah with such a huge change of worlds for him that included two languages Castellano and the official language of Barcelona, Catalan. Danica's response was more less, "What an amazing experience you could give to him!" I thought, yes that is so true! I thought to myself I would have loved to have that experience at ten years old. I couldn't know for sure but had to give it a try. I knew we could always come back to the United States if it didn't work. I left Danica's house with tears streaming down my face. These were tears of happiness because I knew I had to take this risk. I decided that sunny April morning that I would give my current employer my resignation notice at the beginning of June which would be a month in advance and plenty of ample time. That same day later in the afternoon I met up with my lifelong childhood best friend Marla in one of my favorite Chicago neighborhoods Wicker Park and let her know my decision to move to Barcelona. Marla was very positive and reassuring about everything I was conveying to her regarding my plans. My biggest and honestly only concern at this point now was what I was going to do with my car as I still had payments on it. After telling her my concern she jokingly said, "Maybe it will get totaled." I left Marla to have dinner at Piece with two of my high school friends. I was excited to catch up with them and let them know my decision to move to Barcelona. On my way home I was driving on the expressway when suddenly the driver in front of me slammed his brakes! I grasped the steering wheel tightly; I was spinning out of control into the next two lanes doing 360 turns! It was truly a miracle nobody got hurt, and my car didn't hit anyone else's car! The other driver came out after my airbags emerged from the impact, and we both just hugged each other, two strangers just thanking God we were okay.

Let God, let the universe take care of the how and just believe. Needless to say, the car was totaled so there was no more car payment to worry about anymore.

Upon my return from Barcelona, Lucas and I started emailing each other practically every day. The very first email went something like this:

Subject: Hi!!!

Hello Gorgeous!!!!

How are you? Did you all arrive fine? I wish you would have missed the plane so that you could still be in Barcelona. I would have loved that! Are you tired?

I hope you know it was so fantastic! Although, too short but, oh my God, soooooo great!!!

It was too sad for us to leave each other so fast. I want you to know something. I came to the airport after and tried to meet you, but your plane already was on board, so I missed you... what a shame!

I know it could seem strange to you to say this only after two days, but you can be sure that all I told you is right and I'm very sincere and I still swear that you're the most beautiful and wonderful woman I have ever known and who kisses so well, and not only this...

You know, I still have marks of your kisses, and I wish you had bitten me more strongly to leave eternal marks on me...

In particular, you've all my respect, and I'll never disturb you and impose you anything. The only thing I wish to ask you is that you still were as you are. Enjoy life as you know it so well and love your son. I kissssssss you so passionately and give also a kiss to your son whom I like so much although I don't know him yet,

Lucas

My response went along the lines like this: Here is a photo of us from the night we met that Lily took of us of our first kiss,

XOXO, Annie :-)

I would continue to send him emails about how much I was missing him and because he and I were such passionate people I would continue to express my feelings to him like this:

"I want to get lost in your eyes while kissing you slowly, softly, and sensually pulling your bottom lip gently to taste you.....then pressing my lips against your lips strongly and passionately until you feel my desire for you run through your veins."

He definitely brought out the poetic side of me. After my weekend decision to move to Barcelona, I would let Lucas know that I would arrive on my actual birthday, July 2nd. He knew he wasn't the sole reason I was moving there, but he did acknowledge he played some part. We were doing this long-distance dating for three months until I would arrive. We were committed to making this work. Besides countless emails and messages almost every day, we Skyped so much and continued to grow closer and closer. To say my heart ached for him was an understatement.

It was the following Monday of my car accident, and my chest was very sore from the impact of the car crash that my doctor advised I not go in that day to work but to rest. The following day my friend Lily who also worked with me picked me up, so we could go to work together since I didn't have a car now. That same day my manager had a meeting with me and advised me that after two and a half years they had to eliminate my position. Can I tell you how happy I was??? I mean now this is the time of the crisis when the market was crashing but honestly the timing could not have been more perfect! I literally said that it is so okay and that I am alive and happy and if this is the worst thing that happens, I am in good shape! She cried and hugged me while whispering in my ear, "This doesn't feel right." I got home and celebrated with a glass of champagne and toasted to my new chapter! I mean everything was falling in place the minute I decided and committed to my decision! The severance pay I received paid for my airline ticket to Barcelona, a new laptop, and for me to get my TEFL certification: Teaching English as a Foreign Language. All the pieces of the puzzle were fitting perfectly and seamlessly.

My next step was to go to court where my good friend, attorney May would represent me. The judge would allow my son to go out of the country as I had sole custody, and his father Charles would be the summer resident parent where Jeremiah would be with him every summer. During the school year the plan would be that they would Skype all the time to ensure they continued to be in each other's life. Yana would take care of any affairs while I was gone. Lastly, I got a Power of Attorney and a realtor, so everything was covered!

Weeks before I was to leave for Barcelona, I emailed Lucas a poem I had written to him.

From the moment you walked in my life
I never felt things quite so right.
The universe would have us greet in
An Irish pub to meet.
Barcelona of all places is where my heart would suddenly change.
The moment you kissed me my world had changed!
One look in your eyes…. I knew you were mine.
Your kiss made me so weak
I could feel my heart skip a beat.
The night couldn't end so we stayed up in my bed.
Feeling the heat between us as our bodies touched…

God! I wanted you so much!

Kisses of passion, tasting your lips, your hands on my hips.

I wanted to lose control.

Lost in your eyes.....surprised by the night

Every part of my body quenches for more.

You have captivated me and captured my heart!

As time has gone on and I learn more

About this man, the one who took my breath away from the start!

I become more intrigued and amazed at his beautiful soul!

I love him so much and never want to let him go!

I sometimes question, how can this all be?

I then remember how life can be.

Now I await to see you soon,

But see you with even more passion than I have ever known

To give you all.....mind, body, and soul.

He responded to my poem that he was so happy to receive my beautiful and sweet poem and how he already printed it and put it near his bed along with a picture of me. I loved how romantic he was. He continued to tell me how thankful he was for it and in his words:

"You don't cease to surprise me. You know when I received your message that you had written a poem (even before reading the

poem), I felt at the same time so happy. Having a tear of happiness with such a fascination as to the reflection of our love which I don't have any doubt was so spontaneous....wow!!!!!"

A couple of weeks before starting my life in Catalunya, a group of friends and I decided to go skydiving! I thought number one not only has this been on my bucket list since I was a teenager but what a great analogy! I mean I am going to jump out of a perfectly good plane, and I don't know if the parachute will work or if I will break my legs or even die! I mean I was leaving a great life behind and entering a world of unknowns.

I thought, what the heck, "Why not take the leap?"

Chapter 16

Summer Loving - Hello Barcelona, Paris, and Chicago!

It was the evening before I was to leave for Barcelona. I decided I would spend the summer out there at Lucas's apartment while I would be in search of the perfect flat for my son and me. Next on my to-do list was to ensure that Jeremiah would be all set for the new school year. Lots needed to be done before flying my boy across the pond! I was at my friend Sally's house sleeping, over-filled with anticipation as I was hours away from her driving me to the airport. I can't even begin to describe all the nerves and excitement that flooded my soul! I boarded Air France, and I was suddenly on my way! I mean finally after three long months which felt like forever, I would be reunited with my love Lucas!

I arrived the following day early that morning. It was my thirty-third birthday!!! I came out of the terminal, and there he was! Lucas was standing there waiting for me with the biggest smile. My heart was pounding as it echoed through the walls of the airport. We both ran into each other's arms! He couldn't stop kissing me until we got into the taxi, and I kept staring at him saying, "Is this real? Are you really here?" He showed me around the city and introduced me to my very first Clara, a very refreshing Spanish lemon beer if you will. It's definitely one of my favorite things to drink on a hot summer day.

I was quickly finding out that vacationing and living in a new city are two very different experiences. We got to Lucas's apartment, and I got settled in after taking a nice shower after my long flight. I got to meet his vivacious and sweet cat Bubbles. We headed into town gazing in each other's eyes, and at every stop light he'd grab me and kiss me passionately. I had never in my life been with a man so passionate, so open about his PDA. I loved feeling as if I was the only woman in the world that existed when I was with him. That evening we made love for the first time, and I mean at this point it had been eighteen whole months since I had made love with any man. Can I just say, my gosh, it was so worth the wait! We were both so in love, so drawn to each other that the passion in the bedroom that night could only be described as intoxicating. He had all of me and I all of him.

Living in Barcelona was different from my previous vacation experience. I mean for one the apartment Lucas had didn't have a dryer. I know it doesn't sound like a big deal, but for me when he said here are the clothes pins to hang your wet clothes outside, I instantly panicked! I mean strangers would see my delicates? We would go grocery shopping, and I was so used to my fast-paced life back home I would speed through the aisle as if it was a contest, and he was just simply taking his time as a sloth does to get his food. It never occurred to me how conditioned I was to rush at every task at hand. I would actually have to teach myself to slow down like eating, walking, and enjoying moments in lieu of rushing through them. What a concept! Be in the present moment instead of worrying about the next moment.

Tipping in Barcelona was not like in the United States, and

to be frank it took me a whole year to stop over tipping without feeling the guilt. A tortilla in Barcelona I learned wasn't the corn tortillas I was used to back home. A tortilla here would be known as a tortilla de patata, a Spanish egg and potato omelette that could be eaten for breakfast, lunch, dinner or even served as a bocadillo, a Spanish sandwich served usually on a baguette during a merienda. During a merienda most people would eat a light snack at that time around five p.m. It was quite common to see the streets flooded with children after school who were heading home with their sandwich/bocadillo in hand. Another interesting thing was how lunch at the elementary schools for children ranged from an hour and a half to two hours long. I mean in the United States children are lucky if they even get thirty minutes to eat their lunch. Again, things here were much slower. It was about living in the moment. Lunch was always the biggest meal of the day, and dinner started always around nine or ten p.m. There were so many differences, but I was taking it all in.

I didn't know anybody, but Lucas was very excited to introduce me to meet all his friends and coworkers! I remember before leaving Chicago, my friend Sally telling me how she knew a friend of a friend who lived in Barcelona named Katie who was originally from Chicago. Sally was wonderful with connecting us via email. Katie and I were corresponding and decided the week I arrived to meet up for a brief drink. We both wanted it to be brief because I mean what if we didn't connect? Who wants to be stuck for hours with someone you don't connect with? Safe to say upon meeting we instantly hit it off! What was to be a brief drink hour tops quickly turned into roughly eight long hours of laughing and connecting! We were having so much fun that we lost track of time. Katie and I would be friends for life! She would be my first true friendship made here. It only took us to meet in Barcelona!

That first hot and humid summer in Barcelona was filled with endless memories, and my love and I were only getting closer. Lucas had bought his plane ticket to accompany me to the United States to meet my family and friends back home in Chicago and finally meet my son Jeremiah face to face. We were just a couple days shy of heading to Paris first, Lucas's hometown, before I still needed to find an apartment. I didn't know how, but I knew the perfect apartment was coming, and I didn't fret that I possibly only had forty-eight hours left. The apartments in Barcelona often required a two-to-three-month security deposit which for me was extremely hefty considering I had to be cognizant with the limited funds I had. As only the way the universe can conspire, it presented to me the most perfect apartment. The landlords were fine with settling on one month of security deposit to accommodate my budget. It was everything I was looking for besides the over one hundred steps to the top that would be my built-in gym, so I thought! It was situated right across from the elementary school that Jeremiah would attend and start his fifth-grade year in the neighborhood called Poble Sec. Everything was coming together perfectly. I mean that is what happens when you turn your energy and vision into what you want; you will attract that very thing. I was proof that The Law of Attraction was working in my favor. I often have said our faith is tested up to the very last minute. I knew God wanted to play a practical joke on me just as he did with the car crash that happened last April. I mean, of course, God/universe has my back. It's not for me to say when but just know it's all working in my favor on God's time not Annie's time.

During the summer, of course, I missed my baby boy Jeremiah so much! It was the longest we had ever been apart from one another. We would Skype and correspond over email constantly.

Jeremiah!!!!

I miss you soooo much!!! Thinking of you always! Yesterday Lucas and I were watching videos of you from Disney World and your baseball game. A piece of my heart is gone when I am not with you. You mean the world to me. I hope you are enjoying your summer. Sending you soooo much love!!!! Have fun with Yana and everyone this weekend! Can't wait to skype and see you sweet pea!!!!

Love you with all my heart!!! I love being your mom!!!!!
Kisssssssssssses!!!!!!!!!!

All my love, Mommy

Xoxoxox!!!!!

Jeremiah's reply:

I miss you too. I hope you are having fun. I can't wait to see how you're doing. Write back soon.

Sincerely with all my love,

Jeremiah

While I was truly enjoying myself, I couldn't deny the huge hole that was missing in my heart until I could reunite with my boy. I was becoming anxious and knew it would be weeks away before I got to give him the biggest hug ever! I mentally would pinch myself always that I got to be HIS mom, my sweet boy.

It was August when Lucas and I left for Paris, and we stayed in his parents' beautiful Paris apartment right across the street from the stunning Luxembourg Gardens. The integrity and architecture of this apartment was so charming, so Parisian. His parents were in their other home located in Basque Country, Bayonne, France, so we had the whole place to ourselves. There was something so romantic about being there with him in Paris and watching him in his hometown's element. Could I fall even more in love with him? Gasp! We went to the local grocery store nearby and bought so many different types of local exotic cheeses, fresh breads, and an array of delicious French wines. He made me fall in love with camembert cheese, a cheese from northern France. One delicate bite of camembert with a sip of Saint Emilion and then Château Margaux splashed together swooshing all around in my pallet. Mmmmm! Am I in heaven? Delicious doesn't even describe the pairing but to soak up the seconds of taste was a priceless experience!

Lucas took me to so many of the beautiful parks that Paris boasted of---stunning views with sweet kisses along the way. One late summer evening we headed to the Eiffel tower and wrote our names on the tower amongst one of the many millions of names already written. Kissing passionately under the bright lights seemed like being in some sort of movie. I loved him, and the love just wouldn't stop growing! What was happening? I never felt a love like this in my life. I mean our imprints were all over Paris and to be fair any city we touched. To end our trip, he took out his cello and in his Parisian apartment invited me to a concert for one. He played for me there in his living room, and I was mesmerized. His already passionate personality only overflowed when he played. Is there anything he can't do? I was so grateful for Lucas sharing this other side of him. He always made me feel like the luckiest girl on the planet.

The following day we were off to my hometown of Chicago---the best skyline, deep dish pizza, and people in the world! Sorry, I know I may be biased, but this city doesn't disappoint. I needed to ensure that I would give Lucas a proper tour which included the Sears tower stressing to him to ignore that it says Willis Towers as any true Chicagoan would do. We went everywhere, and he was in complete awe. I loved that when we went to the grocery store, he couldn't believe how many options we had here in America. "How many brands of breads do you have in this one aisle?" He said with a bewildered look on his face. It never occurred to me just how many choices and options we as Americans do have. The portion sizes simply just shocked Lucas. I mean he couldn't believe what he was about to sink his teeth into which was the biggest and juiciest triple burger he ever had! This scrumptious burger was the size of his face!

I wanted to make Lucas's first trip to America filled with a lifetime of memories. I decided I would surprise him at one of my favorite Italian restaurants on the northwest side of Chicago called Sabatinos. I called the owners beforehand to ensure that the day of our reservations a surprise would be awaiting him. That evening we arrived at the restaurant, and when Lucas looked up at the restaurant's marquee, there in **BIG BLACK BLOCK** letters flashed on Irving Park Road that read, **"WELCOME TO AMERICA, LUCAS!"** Lucas turned and looked at me and said, "For me?" He was in disbelief with a countenance filled of shock as he was taking it all in. I wanted to be the one to make him feel so special, appreciated, and loved in every way. Inside the restaurant we had a private booth for two awaiting our arrival. He sat next to me rather than across, and we began our dinner sipping on crisp and bubbly champagne followed by a bottle of their best red wine. The violin and guitar player came and played as we ate our pasta to the Italian sounds and melodies of love. It was perfect, he was perfect, and he was all mine.

"Let's go to Hawaii," I said. "I can transport you there." We drove to one of the oldest tiki bars in River Grove, Illinois, just outside Chicago called Hala Kahiki. It is a great place for anyone who has several hours between their flights as it's situated minutes from O'Hare. The vibe is so tranquil, and you really don't feel as if you are in Illinois anymore, and certainly the cocktails take you somewhere. It's as if you are in the state of Hawaii with Hawaiian music playing throughout. This place set a romantic tone, and he was loving all these new experiences!

The best part for me was when Lucas and I arrived at Lily's house. This was the moment I had been anticipating when Lucas would finally meet my Jeremiah! It was amazing not only for me to give my boy the biggest hug ever but introduce him to my love. I have always been protected by who my son would meet. They both hit it off, and Lucas was so wonderful with him! Jeremiah gave us these sweet bracelets he handmade for the both of us. I mean how super sweet! I just was beyond excited to see my baby boy!!

Giving my boy Jeremiah the biggest hug
after not seeing him for weeks!

To top off all this amazing momentum of Lucas's "Welcome to America" tour, my good friend Manny had a welcome home party for us welcoming my boyfriend, Lucas! Manny, who was also like a brother to me, was always the life of the party so him and Lucas hit it off instantly. I along with the rest of our friends standing in Manny's kitchen could not stop laughing as they both were singing loudly and bouncing their contagious and fun energy onto all of us. My friends witnessed the vibrant energy of the love of my life right in front of them---a sneak peek if you will on why they could see how I was so smitten with him. I know all my girlfriends Sally, Steph, Jolene, and May were all smiling ear to ear so happy for me and could transparently see how much in love we both were. They all meant the world to me, and their feedback was necessary! I loved getting lost in watching how effortless Lucas and my friends interacted and got along.

Sally suggested we go to a Korean barbecue restaurant nearby later that week. Lucas was excited to try everything! We all ate so much until our pants were bursting at the seams! It was an amazing, tasty Korean barbecue dinner experience with Sally, Steph, and my love Lucas.

The weeks would continue in Chicago, and Lucas kept meeting more and more important people in my life. Tonight, was going to be an evening of fun karaoking at a little local dive bar. "Lucas, please meet Marla. She is one of my childhood best friends since we were four years old. Oh Lucas! Do you remember the story of the one who said maybe I will get into a car accident when I decided I was moving to Barcelona? This is her!" I said excitedly!

When suddenly my friend since high school Donna firmly looked Lucas in the eye and said with tears streaming down her face,

"You better not hurt her. She has been through enough." Donna truly had helped me so much in my twenties with landing me a job as an Assistant Branch Manager at the bank she worked at and helped me numerous times with watching my son Jeremiah. She was truly rooting for my happiness. Lucas appreciated the love my friends had for me and was grateful he was stepping into my world with open arms.

Lucas decided to grab the microphone and tell the DJ to play Metallica's Enter Sandman. He was rocking that song! The crowd and all my friends there were loving it and loving Lucas! I stood there with the biggest smile. It took me back to our first double date with Lily and John back in Barcelona. That was when Lucas started to sing that same song at our dinner table.

In order to make Lucas's trip even more unforgettable, I made sure he would experience a Chicago Cubs' game in the bleachers. We would purchase our overpriced juicy Chicago hot dogs and icy cold beers while soaking up the energy of the fans. My family including my sister was very happy I was showing him the way! I mean Cubbies were in my family's veins running a very true blue!

Lucas's August was a month-long love affair with Chicago. September crept in, and he had to leave to get back to work in Barcelona. I stayed behind for another couple of weeks in order to finish packing up my townhome and say my goodbyes to my family and friends. Jeremiah and I would be on our way with our seven pieces of luggage! A new chapter for the both of us into an unknown world that was awaiting.

Chapter 17

Life With Lucas

The three of us now were getting adjusted to our new lives together. Lucas and I both wanted to ensure that Jeremiah had all the resources he needed and that he got to have a proper introduction of Barcelona. We set out to all the beautiful parks in Barcelona such as Parc de Montjuic to explore the touristy and lively streets of Las Ramblas and more. Outside of Plaça de Catalunya we decided to sit at a nearby cafe. Jeremiah ordered a hot chocolate and tasty churro. Sitting there with my hair in a messy bun, I couldn't help but be in the moment. My heart, my boy Jeremiah, was now here and next to me there was Lucas, the love of my life. I observed how wonderful Lucas was with Jeremiah and the way Lucas sincerely wanted to get to know my son filled my heart. The two of them had an instant bond and connection. It only made me fall deeper in love with Lucas. He would help with picking up Jeremiah from school, go to basketball games, and spend quality time with him. He always made Jeremiah feel included in whatever we did.

Lucas had never been with a woman who had a child, nor did he have his own, so this was all new territory for him. I loved how he said he was so attracted to my strength for having to raise him. His perspective regarding single moms was one that isn't commonly shared among the masses. For him it was something to be proud of, and I loved that! He knew I was trying to raise a good, strong young man. I always knew my son and I came as a beautiful, packaged deal. How neat to find someone who praises and loves that package! I knew if any man dared to view me having a child as an issue or a speed bump, then that person wasn't for me. It was that simple. I am the mom that never was nervous to tell any man I had a child. Matter of fact, it was one of the first things I would let a man know. I would shout it on the rooftops if I could!

Lucas was seemingly at my apartment more and more, and

it just made sense for him to move in. We discussed on my balcony about trying it. Lucas was nervous as he loved having his own personal space. After much discussion Lucas decided he would take the plunge and advise his landlord he was moving out.

Lucas and I started to get in a groove as a family. One of the things I loved about our evening routine was how we would cook together, have a toast/cheer, and enjoy our company preparing each dish with love, laughter, and kisses. "Lucas, I am going to start peeling this shiny eggplant."

"Your eggplant parm is my favorite." Lucas replied. Suddenly, in the middle of peeling the skin from the eggplant, a worm appeared crawling his way out! Lucas would just laugh and say how fresh the eggplant was! I just thought to myself there should be a warning label with a side effect of heart attack is possible when peeling!

There would be some evenings that Lucas would make some of his yummy French cuisine dishes like Hachis Parmentier. We would sit down together with soft dim candles greeting us at the table and enjoy our family dinner together that we prepared with love. Afterwards, Jeremiah, my little bookworm, would go to his room and read chapter after chapter of his latest book before bed.

Every night before he would fall asleep, we would pray and say, "The Bible is God's word." I always let him know how much I loved him and asked if he wanted to be tucked in like a burrito. Leaving his room with tons of kisses, I would close with "Jeremiah, don't let the bed bugs bite. If they do, hit 'em with a shoe, and they will turn black and blue!" Jeremiah chuckled with the biggest smile as he drifted into a deep sleep.

After my night tuck-ins with Jeremiah, Lucas and I would go out on the terrace and grab a bottle of wine and just talk for hours. One of the things I loved about him was how brilliant and intelligent he was. I loved and cherished our deep conversations. He wasn't just an amazing lover but a deep intellectual and for me that was incredibly attractive. I could stare and talk to him all day!

A couple of months later that November, Lucas and I were lying in bed with our eyes so deeply locked into each other as if we could see far beyond the pupils of our eyes but into our souls. The love was so incredibly deep and profound that we both had never experienced it on such a level. He said he was afraid how much further this love could go because he couldn't believe the height and intensity of our love! To be honest, I didn't think it could exist, not as deep as this.

It was early December on Lucas's birthday where I had planned a surprise weekend getaway for just him and me to Seville, Spain. Jeremiah would stay with my dear friend Katie and her boyfriend David. Jeremiah liked hanging out with them, and David was like an older brother to Jeremiah. So the weekend was a win win! I absolutely loved exploring this city with Lucas. Throughout the weekend I had other birthday gift surprises, and he was ever so grateful. We would walk in the bar, and he would sing out loud per usual as he and I had that same energy and zest for life! The people of Seville singing back and just the liveliness of the city was magnetic and infectious!

One evening we decided to get tickets to a Flamenco show.

While watching the intensity and power of the dance, tears started to fall down my cheek. The strong and heartfelt performance between the two dancers was exceptional. I loved the culture and heart here in Seville. The following day we decided to take a romantic carriage ride through the town which included endless kisses throughout this trip that made for the perfect getaway.

In the months to come Jeremiah, Lucas, and I would travel to the lively Lisbon, Portugal, and the mountainous and stunning Andorra. We also were fortunate to spend time with Lucas's beautiful, warm, and loving family in one of the Basque cities of Bayonne, France, for Christmas which included exploring the breathtaking Penedès mountains and more! A month later we were off to Rome, Italy, for Jeremiah's 11th birthday. I have to admit watching my son explore other countries, languages, and cultures just made me so happy. I loved that we got to experience creating beautiful memories like this together. Jeremiah particularly loved Italy---the colosseum, the Roman emperors dressed up outside, and the pizza. Oh! How he loved the pizza that was bigger than his head! Jeremiah also very much loved the snow; it's as if mother nature granted him a temporary gift. Rome had a huge snowfall for the first time in twenty-five years! "Mom, look!" Jeremiah shouted as he stuck his tongue out to taste the down pouring of tiny white snowflakes. We were so unprepared! Our shoes were drenched. The city shut down, and people who were under twenty-five years of age and who had never experienced or seen snow in their life began to take pictures on the streets. It was magical! By afternoon, the snow was completed gone. It was as if that morning was just a dream. Ah, Italy! You are surely full of surprises!

Italy is also the place where their yummy gelatos do not disappoint! You almost want to take your sweet time savoring each lick of ice cream that seems to precisely know how to taunt your taste buds perfectly. No trip to Rome is ever complete until we made sure to throw a coin into the Trevi Fountain. Legend has it that if you do, you are sure to return to Rome! So this was definitely a MUST DO! How could we not come back to this gorgeous, culture filled country?

Coming back to Barcelona was wonderful because I had a job I loved. I taught English at an academy in Barcelona. My students ranged from as young as five years old and to elder adult professionals like nurses, architects, etc. Gosh, did I love them all! With each day I started to feel as if Barcelona was where I belonged.

Chapter 18

My Solo Adventure in Greece

Summer was approaching, and it was the month of June when Lucas was going to Cadiz, Spain, for a seminar he was going to be speaking at, and I didn't want to stay home while he was away. Instead, I opted to go on a solo adventure. Oh, the choices! I decided why not Athens, Greece? I can go for a few days and explore their history, culture, and more!

Off to the airport I went! It was time for me to put myself out there; traveling alone was a great way. While I was waiting at the airport's boarding area, there sat a lovely woman I started chatting with from Bombay, India. My mind automatically drifted away thinking how one day I want to travel to India. We all had to start boarding the plane. Next to me was a woman heading to a wedding from New Jersey. This was just the start of many different people from many walks of life I would encounter. It was so nice getting to know them both; all I could think was that this trip was off to an amazing start!

I got in a taxi on my way to Hotel Novotel. I was pleasantly delighted with the amazing hospitality they displayed. I got to my room, stepped out onto the balcony, and took in a deep breath of fresh air. I was ready to explore Athens!

Roaming around the cobblestone streets taking in my surroundings, I suddenly stumbled upon a charming and bustling restaurant called Taveren Vigantino. I found a nearby table outside where I could enjoy this gorgeous day. The sun's rays gently beaming across my face as I started to sip on an icy cold Mythos. This yummy Hellenic lager beer from Greece was perfect as I did some people watching. I just can't stop smiling and mentally giving thanks for how grateful I am to be here. Traveling solo really made me truly take in everything, all my surroundings which I knew was one of the great benefits of being here by myself. I walked all over town and explored the museums, the Acropolis, and so much more.

The history here is so rich, and I wanted nothing more than to soak it all up!

The very next thing I decided to do was to go to Melissinos Art, The Poet Sandal Maker, of course! This sandal shop is a place where art and poetry as well as custom sandals are made. Yes, custom made just for you! They have made custom sandals for Sophia Loren, Jackie Onassis, The Beatles, Barbara Streisand, and more! The only thing was I couldn't exactly find the shop. I searched and searched and still no dice! I was lost and decided to give the shop a call to see how close or for that matter how far away I was. Needless to say, I was nearby---just blocks away, and the gentleman in the shop was so kind to come down the street to get me. I looked at all my choices that they could make for me on the spot. I decided to get the Melite, also known as the Jackie O. They measured my feet and began the process. Voila, my own custom Grecian sandals! How cool is that? My favorite purchase in Athens. My only regret after leaving the shop was how I wish I purchased another pair. I'd be back one day again to get my Gladiator/Cleopatra sandals that kept whispering buy me, too. In the meantime, my Jackie O's would do.

The following evening, I decided to head to the rooftop of a beautiful and romantic restaurant that was overlooking the Acropolis. It was stunning! I looked to my left and then to my right, and I found myself surrounded by couples and candle lit tables of couples upon couples simply gazing into each other's eyes. I followed the host that led me to my seat with no date to accompany me. My waiter approached me and asked if I was waiting for anyone and I said, "No, it's a table for one, and I'd like a glass of champagne please."

"Oh", he replied. Then proceeded to say, "What are we celebrating?"

I said with a smirk and paused for a brief second looking into his eyes, "Me".

He smiled back ear to ear and proceeded to pop that bubbly for me. I love that I am celebrating me now! Yes, that's right, ME!!!! I am right now at this very moment loving the life I have recreated for myself. The surge of empowerment I feel is so liberating! I believe everyone deserves to pour their own version of champagne whatever it may be and celebrate who you are, where you came from, where you are going, and what you have overcome and toast to beautiful and fabulous you! In doing so, you will feel such empowerment. Here I am with a dainty glass of bubbly champagne in my right hand overlooking the Acropolis toasting to how far I have come. I say to myself that I find beauty in all, and in that the beauty of experiences awakens me. I am romancing myself in a way every woman/man should romance herself/himself. It's a full moon tonight under the Acropolis as I slowly admire this historic beauty with every sip of crisp champagne that hits my pallet. The sun starts to set creating an even more inviting ambiance over my romantic table for one. All I can do as I sit here and continue to be in awe with my current view is to feel God's goodness that I am happy finally with just me. For one reason or another we often believe in order to have these types of experiences we need a friend, a partner, someone. I challenge anyone to create a day where you go to a romantic place and put yourself out there, order a glass of champagne, and celebrate you!

Later that evening, I wanted to be near the neighborhood where my hotel was. I found a little local cafe around the corner filled with nothing but locals. The bartender told me she was from Russia and spoke very little English. The rest of the filled cafe/pub was from Greece. It is a beautiful thing being alone, being vulnerable, and putting myself out there when I don't speak the language. However, in the coolest and craziest way we all somehow communicated like a game of charades along with my handy translation book. The whole cafe is intrigued that I am trying so hard to speak their language as they know I am an American woman originally from Chicago. One by one they started to buy me a drink called Ouzo. Then another ouzo and another and they seemingly don't stop their generosity! If you don't know what Ouzo is get ready to have some hair on your chest! You have to sip it slowly, and I mean slowly because it's very strong; it is basically a dry anise-flavored aperitif which almost reminds me of the candy Good and Plenty or a licorice. This is a true staple here in Greece. As the night went on, we started to get up from our chairs and bar stool. Who would've thought that the owner was going to teach me how to do a traditional Greek dance! Um, YES, PLEASE! I was loving every second of this!!! I mean I could have done what a lot of tourists do and go to the most crowded and touristy places, but I chose to throw myself amongst the locals, and it was the best decision ever. Travel is truly what you make it, and sometimes not having a play-by-play agenda gives you all the room to allow other opportunities that you could never have planned for. What a wonderful trip Greece was for me. This marked my two rich years of traveling solo, and I wouldn't trade those experiences for the world!

It was time for me to get on the plane and head back to Barcelona. The whole plane ride there I was filled with gratitude, a common reoccurrence. This trip was preparing me, preparing me for something more. It was going to be a gift to my future self that I can be fine alone and just me will always be enough.

Chapter 19

The Return

I landed back in Barcelona after a very refreshing three-day

trip to Greece, waiting for Lucas to meet me at the airport. I grabbed

my luggage and headed to arrivals waiting with anticipation to run

into Lucas's arms! Minutes pass by, and all of a sudden, a deep

feeling in the pit of my belly starts saying "something is

wrong". That feeling was only getting stronger as gentle whispers

were entering into my subconscious. I politely tucked those thoughts

and feelings back away. I mean silly me---surely everything is fine.

I waited for what felt like forever and still no Lucas. Maybe he got

wrapped up in his work, or maybe there was an accident on the

freeway? I mean every trip I ever took he would always be on the other side waiting for me, but somehow, I knew something about today was different. I proceeded to text him, "Where are you?" and he texted me back! Thank God! Then I started to read what his response was.

I am not coming.

He continued to text me on how hard it was for him not to be there at the airport and just to leave me there without any warning whatsoever, but he just couldn't do it anymore. He couldn't be in this relationship any longer. I wanted to collapse right there in the airport! I thought to myself when I get home, I will talk to him, and we can make this all better. Surely, he can't be serious! The taxi drive from the airport home was filled with anxious anticipation just to talk to him! Subconsciously, I was shouting, "Step on the gas pedal!" It was very late in the evening when I went up our one hundred plus steps to the top of our apartment. I unlocked the door, and as I pushed the door open, the first thing I noticed besides the pitch darkness and the invisible guards with machine guns to my heart was his cat Bubbles and all of Lucas's personal items were gone. Lucas and his cat had left. My heart is now in more pieces than any complex jigsaw puzzle could ever count. I wanted to die of heartbreak. I called my only friend Katie in Barcelona that wasn't connected to him in any way. Katie rushed and jumped in her car to come get me. She finds me there on the floor trying to get the words out of my mouth as I felt I was having a panic attack barely able to breath. She wasn't going to let me be there alone, and my gosh, am I forever grateful. I stayed with her the next few days with hope that I could somehow mend my broken and inconsolable heart.

Days later I sent an email to Lucas:

You will never know how I felt coming home to our apartment empty. No Bubbles, our crazy cat to make sure he would run out the door and drive you nuts chasing him! No Lucas to wrap his arms around me. My heart was being ripped into a million pieces. It felt like an army of men with their guns that were waiting for me to come in and blow me to pieces. I am in pure devastation. I know I am alive, but mentally I am dead. My heart beats but with emptiness. I have eyes that see but are full of sorrow. I am a walking zombie, and I haven't eaten or slept, and when I close my eyes, I close them so I can imagine you next to me. I close my eyes imagining your lips will press against mine once again. I close my eyes imagining feeling your body against me. I close my eyes to feel you make love to me. Finally, when I do dream, it is of you I am happy that at least I was able to see you. I know this is crazy, but I can't explain it any better...

Here I am almost as to what seems as having an obsessed state of mind. All I could do was think what was going through his mind? Why would he want to end the beautiful love we have? How could he walk away? Why am I not good enough for him? WAIT, I AM GOOD ENOUGH! So why? I couldn't stop pondering while replaying Coldplay's "I Miss You" repeatedly.

I did so much reflection and soul searching as to why and how this could even end. I realized that I so badly wanted to control the narrative of our story that I slowly somehow was still managing to sabotage our relationship. I couldn't believe that after Charles and my Dark Knight and all the work I did on me that this happened. I mean Lucas crossed my path at the perfect time, and he was the one who would show me the way a woman should be treated and loved. So how could this be the way our story would end? Indeed, Greece was preparing me that I am just fine being alone.

Reflecting and realizing that as the more time passed during the course of our relationship, the more I found my heart becoming more and more invested. This to me was the equivalent of having a seat at the high rollers' table at a fancy casino gambling with even higher odds. What if I lose this amazing love? I couldn't imagine there would be no us. In a subconscious state of panic as our love got deeper, I started to internally feel worried throughout the course of the relationship. My insecurities were getting the best of me. There were a few instances where I can recall I was pushing him away although not my intention. I remember we were in Toulouse, France, visiting some of his family members, and that was when things in our relationship suddenly took a turn in my opinion. We had an argument, and what I do remember from it was the feeling of I messed up. One night at home while having a candlelit dinner, I broke down and just cried telling him how sorry I was for testing him. He expressed time and time again to stop testing him. The thing is every time I tested him that little inner voice would say to me don't do it! STOP! I knew that to control is not to love. Regardless, if he leaves, we are free to make our own choices. I just didn't want our love story to end. I wish I could have not let the insecurities I had ruin and bring the very thing I didn't want to happen.

He tried to end things with me a few months back, weeks before our one-year anniversary, and I begged him to give us another chance. We agreed to give us another shot and sealed it with a kiss. Weeks prior to going to Greece Lucas and I brought Jeremiah to the airport so he could be with his dad for the summer. Jeremiah was about to go through security, and as we hugged and said goodbye, Lucas gave Jeremiah a beautiful letter. He read it before leaving us. In the letter I must admit that it almost felt as if he was saying goodbye to Jerry. He loved Jeremiah so much, and Jeremiah loved him right back. Here we are now just weeks later, and it really was over. I had a feeling on the plane when I was coming back from Greece. I could feel in the pit of my stomach that there was going to be a change on the horizon. I just didn't know what. Lucas had to leave the way he did because I didn't want to believe what he was feeling. No matter how hard he tried, it wasn't working for him. Truthfully, I should have accepted it months ago and gracefully let him go.

I should have heard his cry as I had gone through my own personal journey to find me. Lucas really wanted to focus on him, and at the time I thought how selfish he was. However, to be fair, it truly was my broken heart speaking. It's like in the movie *Sex and the City*. In the end Samantha says she does love Smith but loves herself more. How could I blame Lucas for wanting to work on the relationship he has with himself first? He did teach my future self a very valuable lesson in that. I just didn't know it at the time.

My world never felt more over, but for some strange reason I knew deep down that this too shall pass, and I would indeed be whole again.

Chapter 20

Summer Encounters

I was so grateful that I had Katie here in Barcelona. She and I have created such a strong and deep friendship since the first day we met. Thank God for her! However, it was time I put myself out there and start meeting other people while creating new friendships that excluded Lucas. Suddenly, I remembered Barcelona had tons of different MeetUp groups where you could network and meet people. What a great concept! So, I did just that.

It was a hot summer night in July, and I decided to go on one of the planned activities. One of the MeetUps that was being organized was going to be held at a chiringuito with dinner, drinks, and music on the beach. Chiringuitos are quite popular in Barcelona which is basically a bar and/or restaurant on the beach. I was going!

This seemed as if it could be a lot of fun. So, I reserved my spot online and got ready that evening to put myself out there. Arriving at the groups table that had the backdrop of the Mediterranean Sea, I found my seat. I sat there listening to the DJ compete to the sounds of the sea just jamming away! The energy was high! I needed some good energy coming my way! Sitting to the left of me was a woman, a local named Mercedes and to my right, a woman named Apple, and I don't mean the fruit or iPhone. Apple was an architect who was from the Philippines living in San Francisco but was traveling before permanently changing her address somewhere in Hong Kong. These two would be my first friends that I would make in Barcelona after my post break up. Mercedes had this incredible smile and this positivity for life! We both believed in the Law of Attraction, so it was no surprise it was meant to be that we would meet. Her English wasn't the best, but it gave me all the opportunity in the world to practice my Spanish with her and help her with her English. She simply was just so lovely and a beautiful, radiant soul.

Now Apple and I had this instant connection that I can't even describe or put into words except to say the stars aligned that night on that sandy beach. Apple and I decided since she only had roughly about a week left in Barcelona that we should continue to hang out before her departure. I would show her all my favorite spots in town! We truly enjoyed mingling with all the locals as they were just so much fun to be around. Monday nights for me meant being at my favorite Irish Pub located across from the historic Sangrada Familia called Michael Collins where I was nicknamed "Chicago". "Hey Chicago!" "What will it be tonight Chicago?" It was my spot where the vast majority of the bartenders were from the vibrant country of Ireland. This place ensured there were no shortages of laughs, drinks, and engagement from the locals. Spending time here with Apple was so therapeutic for me and the best thing to keep my mind off my broken heart. She was looking forward to having this time before settling in with her boyfriend who already left for their new apartment in Hong Kong. Apple was soon experiencing what was already unveiled to me that Barcelona is a truly magical city. In hindsight, Apple arrived in Barcelona thinking she knew exactly who she was as did I and so many of us expats. The truth is it was only the beginning of a search to find ourselves in ways and layers we never could expect. You see Apple, too, was living by a script of rules like myself that she constantly felt guilty if she didn't live by. Personally, for me my past consisted of living under strict Fundamental Baptist rules such as divorce not being an option or God forbid you danced to rock music, etc. Apple had this immense pressure to live up to her family's expectations. Follow that invisible rule book set for her life. She indeed was searching to find herself but just didn't know it yet.

Soul searching who you are can be summed up or compared to a sleeping dragon. Let me explain. We all know that a dragon is known for its fierceness, nobleness; it's supernatural powerful wings that can soar effortlessly and more! However, what if this majestical creature with all these admirable characteristics was just sleeping away, passing each minute through life not exemplifying what gifts it truly has? Perhaps not even having any idea as to what gifts it has externally and internally? Slowly becoming a sleeping dragon that is chained and locked or otherwise trapped figuratively and or literally speaking? How sad that this could even be a possibility! This is just like so many of us and our souls.

I was born in the year of the dragon according to the Chinese zodiac as a fire dragon nevertheless which is known for their intelligence and being social. Dragon signs supposedly have breakthroughs in their middle years and enjoy prosperity later in life. That sounded very familiar to me as I can personally concur that my mental shift/breakthrough, one of many to follow, would first happen a couple of months before I was turning thirty-one years old. It was when I finally started living! I mean truly LIVING and on purpose!!! I don't mean it's when I figured it all out, but it was when I took responsibility as to how I was going to show up in my life. However, before then, I was the definition of a sleeping dragon, going through the motions on the outside but dying inside and trapped and not living the life I thought could ever be possible for someone like me. I grew up with not much, but that little girl always had BIG, BIG DREAMS!

I was very sad that it was time to say goodbye to Apple as she was about to fly to London before Hong Kong to visit her brother. In such a short time getting to know Apple, it was as if she was the woman version of my soulmate---the apple of my eye. I knew our friendship would continue no matter the distance.

In the midst of a broken heart, you can continue to die, or you can choose to start living. I was beyond grateful to have such a huge support system with my friendship circle regardless of the distance.

Every August since I moved my life to Barcelona, I would visit Chicago for the month to see my family and friends. This particular August everyone thought for sure I would be heading back to my hometown permanently after my breakup with Lucas. However, that was not the case. To be honest, the thought didn't even cross my mind as an option. I felt I was just getting to know the bones of this city and feel its pulse.

Still feeling like a zombie and numb from feelings, I was carrying a heart that was so severely shattered bleeding to death, or so it felt. My loving mom and dad reassured me that I would be fine, and life would go on. My younger sister and my aunt were all reaching out to ensure I was okay. My friends were a rock to me when I wanted to die.

It's truly so important to have friends who are rooting for you, who are lending shoulders to lean on, and who will always have your back. My circle of friends is loyal and fierce. My friends had virtual X-ray vision glasses on and could see through and feel the pain in my heart. If I ever needed the support of my family and friends, it was definitely now.

Here is an introduction to these **nine** ladies who rallied around me BIG **back home!**

Marla: My first childhood best friend and sister from another mister since I was four years old. She always had a way to put things into perspective when perhaps mine was over analyzed. She was the one when life didn't make sense would remind me we would always be family no matter where we are in life.

Yana: My second childhood best friend who again was also like a sister to me since we were six years old and who always has been there for me my whole entire life. She was always someone I could count on no matter what time of day it was. I always knew she would be there. There are no words to express that type of bond we have sister to me since we were six years old and who always has been there for me my whole entire life. She was always someone I could count on no matter what time of day it was. I always knew she would be there. There are no words to express that type of bond we have after all these years.

Danica: Yana's cousin who was ten years older than us and was like an older sister to me. She always made sure I was okay. Her heart is so big! I am grateful for her being there for me during times I needed it the most throughout my whole life. Priceless!

Tania: A friend I met many years ago when we worked for one of the biggest law firms in the world. I asked her if she would go to lunch with me. She said yes and the rest is history! She is the definition of what being a loyal friend is---beautiful inside and out! In my low times she and her husband have been there for me in some of my darkest hours. I could never repay them except to say I am eternally grateful!

Val: A friend who I met through Lily's husband, John, in my late twenties at a barbecue. She was my Starbucks buddy as she was studying for school and I for the TEFL exam. She has always been the friend that when you leave her presence, you just feel better. I have appreciated her friendship more than she will ever know! She is a friend that I know when I need someone to lean on and talk to, she will always be there.

Steph: My beautiful Serbian friend who I met through Sally. The first seconds upon meeting there was an instant connection! We were both about energy attracting like energy, and our friendship has grown and soared since! She has always been the one with encouraging words that would massage my soul.

Mona: A friend I have known since we were in seventh grade. We had the same strict fundamental Baptist rules, graduated high school together, and more! We lost touch in our twenties, but when she showed up on my doorstep, we picked up right where we left off. Grateful doesn't even describe how thankful I am for her friendship. She has always believed in me which has meant the world.

Lastly, **Lily** and **Emily**: Two beautiful souls that I met at different times of my life---loyal, loving, and presently there no matter what.

So much of my life in my thirties has been exemplified because of the friendships with these two.

These ladies were just a handful of my friends who consistently messaged me words of encouragement and breathed back life into me including my baby sister. She always made sure I was okay no matter if we lived miles apart. I love her so much for that. Having just spent the month of August in Chicago with them and a handful of other beautiful friends, I was armored and ready to fly back to Barcelona. I knew this would be a new chapter, and I was ready whether I wanted to believe it or not.

Chapter 21

Single and Ready to Mingle!

Year two and Jeremiah and I were heading back to Barcelona! Jeremiah would be going into the sixth grade and into a private school called Cor Mar Gràcia in lieu of his former public school that was across the street when we lived in the neighborhood of Poble Sec. We also ditched our one hundred plus stair apartment for a first-floor apartment in the lively area of Gràcia. A new chapter was emerging, and new experiences would begin.

My good friend Emily from Upland, California, who I had met on my solo trip to Europe a couple of summers ago was flying out this September to visit me. I was ever so grateful that she was coming! Emily, one of my close best friends, always checked on me and made sure I was okay. When she finally did arrive from across the pond, she did everything she could to get me out of my uninviting lingering funk. We were both single and ready to mingle. A fun and vibing place was one of my favorite dance clubs called Magic. Magic played a lot of eighties music and was only ten euros which included the entrance fee and a beer along with a shot or one spirit of your choice. Magic had such an incredible energy that wouldn't really get sardine packed with locals of all ages flooding in until around midnight. This place would go on into the wee hours of the morning, but it was always a sure good time! An extrovert's dream! We decided to head there.

On the crowded dance floor Emily had met a guy named Julian who was with several friends. Inviting us over to join them, I also got to meet Joseph. Months later New Year's Eve, I would meet Monte, Joseph's brother; little did I know that these three would become like brothers to me: Julian, Joseph, and Monte. I loved these three tons! I was like one of the guys with them, and we just flowed so effortlessly. Our nights out in Barcelona could only be described as endless belly laughs of fun! My friend Julian was amazing to my son, always encouraging Jeremiah to learn Brazilian

Jiu-Jitsu and inviting him to go to his dojo. He would partner up with him during classes and show him the way. I loved the bond I had with my Barcelona brothers. Shortly after that night of meeting them, my friend Emily and Julian would start a long-distance relationship. My newfound brothers also had a friend who was from Brazil named Johan, and my friend Julian was very persistent that he and I go on a blind date. I thought to myself why not? So later that week, Johan and I met for drinks, and let's just say my heart was racing a zillion seconds per beat when I saw him. His smile, his eyes, and his chiseled physique made me melt. Are all the men in Brazil this gorgeous? I mean he was perfect. Then when he kissed me, I was weak in the knees and grew faint to say the least. I was slowly coming out of my breakup coma. Thank you, Johan!

Things got even better! Apple reached out to me. She told me that she and her Dutch boyfriend decided to go their separate ways after four years of being together. Hong Kong was no longer a go! She explained to me that the last place where she was the happiest was when we had that week together in Barcelona. So, she packed her bags along with her broken heart and was moving here for an undisclosed amount of time! She stayed with Jeremiah and me for about a week before she found a place of her own with new roommates. I was beyond thrilled to have my better half back!

Apple and I decided to head to one of our hangout pubs that was just blocks from my apartment in Gràcia called Gato Negro. I loved everyone who worked there! First there was La Reina; well, that was the nickname I gave her meaning "The Queen". She was from the Dominican Republic and had such a radiant energy. Olen and Oscar, both from Senegal, always wore smiles for miles! I knew I would become good friends with these three. This particular night I went to the bar to order myself a drink in singing form, of course, when a woman standing to the left of me heard me and started laughing. She was from the city of Lleida, located in the northeastern Catalonian region and was now living in Barcelona. She had a vibrant energy about her! Larissa was also an actress and a regular at Gato Negro. She had a crush on Olen whom I nicknamed Smiley. I was rooting for those two! After my singing order was placed, we started talking, and the rest is history! The beginning of a beautiful friendship. Soon after that Apple wanted to take Spanish classes and found a school that was a few blocks away from where she lived. She decided to take a walk over and inquire how she could sign up. While entering the building, there was an elevator, an ancient one that looked as if it had its last run. The language school was located on the fourth floor in a very old building in the neighborhood of Eixample. Apple was standing in front of this tiny, rickety, and bit temperamental elevator where only a maximum of three people could fit. At last, finally the squeaky doors started to open. There was also a man standing next to Apple who went in before her. Apple then proceeded to get into the elevator, and that's when this gentleman's body odor immediately smacked her right in the face. This is also the same time the elevator decided to stop working! She was trapped inside with this man exuding smells that were not in her favor not knowing what to do. Suddenly, what looked like an angel arrived at the lobby and saw her panicked face as she was struggling with the metal bars that were keeping her trapped in. This angel was Susan from Denmark. Susan asked Apple if she needed help. Apple replied frantically, "Yes, please!" She kept doing her best to get the barred fence to unlock and free her. Finally, she did! A million thanks Apple said to Susan. Apple and Susan proceeded to go up the staircase in lieu of the now broken elevator. They quickly realized they were going to the same destination as she wanted to sign up for Spanish classes, too. They both were in line and started talking when she asked Apple what she was doing afterwards. Susan had a friend who was supposed to meet her but ended up cancelling so she wanted to know if Apple could have coffee with her after at the Starbucks near Placa d' Urquinaona. They spent hours chatting. Days later Apple would introduce me, and that is how I met my beautiful and lifelong friend Susan. Susan was a spitting image of Angelina Jolie in my opinion. As time went on, Susan introduced her friend Chrissy to Apple and me who also was from Denmark. Chrissy had the most perfect features. She would share and entertain us all with her stories of dating women in Barcelona. Our tribe of friends and circle was growing!

My sadness was fleeing quicker than the speed of lightning, and my zest for life was back! I was loving my life here in Barcelona! In fact, I loved being single! It was fun, liberating, and freeing!

Chapter 22

A Very Catalan Christmas and New Year

Christmas in Barcelona without the snow was still so magical. The town was lit and definitely had everyone, even Scrooge, in a festive mood! Jeremiah and I had always had a Christmas tradition since he was five years old where we would cut down our Christmas tree from a tree farm in Spring Grove, Illinois. We would vote which one we liked the best and saw it down. Hayride, hot chocolate, and homemade doughnuts were all part of our yearly tradition. We set out into town near the Sangrada area to find the perfect fresh cut tree. Christmas in Barcelona is not complete without ensuring you get a Caca Tio, basically translating to Uncle Poop. It's a log that "poops" out candy. You will see children hitting it with a stick where a blanket is covered over the log, and parents fill the back end with treats. It is quite comical to watch especially with the Christmas market stalls of different sized Caca Tio's on the streets and little kids running up to them and hitting them with so much excitement! I always got such a big laugh out of that! It only made sense for us to join in and buy our very own Caca Tio, too! We found the perfect spot next to our freshly cut tree. Our Christmas Eve was wonderful with just the two of us. The following day we were off to celebrate Christmas with Larissa and her family in Lleida. Jeremiah and I were greeted with big open arms! The kitchen was filled with every food imaginable! "Please keep those gambas (prawns) with their beaded eyes away from me!" I replied with a beating heart. Her family laughed how ridiculous it seemed that I didn't love this delicacy. Spanish wine kept pouring and more and more family members kept coming. Jeremiah was having fun playing video games with Larissa's cousins that were close to his age. The table was set, and we all gathered together, grateful to share a Catalan Christmas with one beautiful family. There we gathered in a circle with Larissa's grandmother leading the way with a silver spoon stroking up and down the empty ridged alcohol glass bottle while leading in song! It was amazing! I was just clapping to the beat and loving the energy! It was a special Christmas I will always remember that I got to spend with my son.

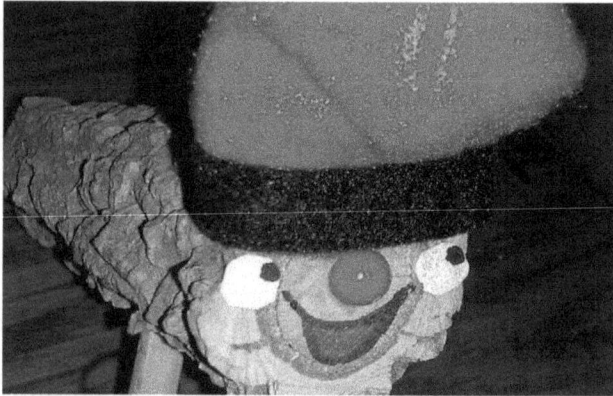

Our purchased smiling Caca Tio.

The few days before New Year's Eve, Lily and Jeremiah's best friend, her son Jack, flew in from Chicago to celebrate and ring in the New Year with us and my friends. Lily and Jack would stay with us for a couple of weeks. Jeremiah was ecstatic and so was I! Prepping for my guests to arrive NYE making my tortilla de patatas, I ensured the bubbly was chilled and ready to go! Festivity feels were all in place for a NYE to remember.

Apple, Susan, Larissa, Julian, Joseph, and Monte Joseph's

brother, have all arrived! My living room was named the Rock Star Lounge because of the many fun social gatherings we would have here from dinners, watching movies, drinks, and laughs. Rock Star Lounge was the place to be. Soon everyone started to come one by one with a dish and spirit ready to count down the evening together!

A tradition, also a superstition in Spain and Catalonia, is that we would all participate along with the rest of Barcelona in the eating of twelve grapes at midnight. It isn't dared to risk the coming year by not participating! I went to the market and ensured each person had a nicely packaged twelve juicy, green grapes. It's the first bell ring! We quickly pop the first grape in our mouth! Bell ring two! Another grape in our mouth! Feeling proud for devouring all twelve plump and juicy green grapes with each ring of the bell which ensured good luck for the New Year, we laughed hysterically as we completed the task.

We each began to write on a separate piece of paper our dreams for the New Year. We rolled it up and put it in an empty wine bottle. We were going to go to the Mediterranean Sea and throw it in the ocean. After the countdown, we did just that! Jack was a couple years older than Jeremiah, a young teenager, so they hung out at the house while the rest of us went to finish celebrating nearby my apartment with our party favors and dancing! It was a New Year to remember!

I couldn't help but love indulging myself in the culture here. I had made a new life here and was discovering who I was more and more.

Chapter 23

Atlas of Friends

Occasionally, Apple and I would reminisce about how it was to have a good steady income back in the USA considering how low our wage was in Barcelona. We remembered the days of free-flowing champagne! One day we said, one day.

Emily was back visiting again myself, and her new beau Julian. Apple, Susan, Emily, and I decided to have a girls' night out in town. We stumbled into a crowded cute place waiting to order our drinks at the bar. As I looked to the left of me, there stood a beautiful woman with long black hair and fair pale porcelain skin holding what looked like champagne with a strawberry grasping tightly on the rim of her flute. I approached her and said in Spanish, "What are you drinking?"

She replied, "I don't speak Spanish. English?"

"Yes!" I exclaimed. "I am American and you?"

She replied that she went by the nickname AJ and that she was Turkish from Istanbul. AJ's drink in hand was a yummy glass of bubbly Cava. This was the Spanish version of champagne as Prosecco is to Italy. I introduced her to our group of friends. Reminding Apple of our earlier conversation regarding champagne. "Cava for everyone in our group please!" I shouted to the bartender.

AJ invited Apple and me to come over for drinks and appetizers that following week. She said she was excited to introduce us to her new friend she met in her Spanish class who moved here from London named Robin. Robin was a beautiful slender woman with gorgeous brown curly hair and the perfect caramel complexion. Little did we know she would complete our circle of friends. Apple, Robin, and I would now be known as the Three Musketeers!

Our growing circle were all single and new to this international dating scene. Single and living in Barcelona, I had no idea the best was yet to come and that this new circle of friends would forever change my life. They would share with me an amazing journey to what the vast majority of women are searching for---some women who just went through a breakup, others just simply trying to find themselves, and the rest on a quest to search for something deeper and more meaningful in life. We came from all different backgrounds, ages, and cultures from the United States, Asia, Middle East, South America, Caribbean, and North and South of Europe! What a gift to share our single journeys here in Barcelona.

Dating in Barcelona could be summed up in so many ways! If you asked Apple, she would say, "Easy come, easy go." It is a place where it is so easy to meet people. Everyone loves to go out, they are friendly, and there are loads of good-looking people. At the same time, it is not so easy because the vast majority of people are not willing to commit to anything serious. Locals say it is this way because they are so used to the transient environment that they are wary to. Apple would say there are loads of expats, and I would agree. There are expats from all over the world so the locals may have a point. One thing we all could agree on was that dating in Barcelona was a wild ride that none of us would ever forget!

This Valentine's Day was going to be unlike any other. We were going to do this right and on our terms! We each selected a name from a bowl that would be our secret Valentine. Our single Valentine party would be held at none other than the Rock Star Lounge, of course.

I am a hopeless romantic. Valentine's Day for some is just another day, but for me, someone who loves LOVE loves it, it was special. I felt so blessed to share the love of friendship in my home where Jeremiah was the honorary male guest exception. My friends loved giving him all the attention in the world. We had a yummy potluck and endless wine and exchanged our gifts only to find who our secret Valentine was. Robin was mine, and I enjoyed shopping for my fierce and fiery dear friend!

We commenced the evening with fake Valentine tattoos and watched movies on the sofa. It was lovely, and we didn't need a partner to justify this day. We only needed each other.

Chapter 24

H + H = H to The Second Power

How do you know when you are with the one? After a long night of pondering over a certain someone, my buddy Apple and I had a very interesting conversation. Dating in Spain (Catalunya) proved to be interesting because there were so many cultural differences that were foreign to me as an American. I was still occasionally seeing my Brazilian Johan. He still had a way with making my heart race a zillion seconds per beat every time that I was in his presence. After every kiss, I would continue to long for more, almost like a drug to me. I knew it was all lust, but he was the greatest distraction from my broken heart. Every time we got together. we enjoyed each other's company, and his smile, that smile was like a Colgate commercial, just perfect! My heart was happy with him, and he was the absolute antidote I needed to permanently get over Lucas, which I did. My head absolutely thought differently of Johan. It's like a school of fish streaming towards my brain waves whispering, "He is not good enough for you. You deserve better. Too many pie slices are missing." These were the thoughts and arguments my brain was having with my heart. How often do we have these conflicts? When our heart and head are out of sync with one another? I think it happens more often than not. I mean my heart was desperately wanting to deny my brain's illusions. At least that is what I was hoping for.

Johan and I were not monogamous by any means. It was understood we were dating other people as we both were in no place of settling down at this point. I wanted to be single and have the freedom that came with that role. Dating other men than Johan was almost the complete opposite experience. Perfect on paper! They had the amazing career, education, ambition, and intelligence--- someone Mom and Dad would be proud their daughter was with. However, my heart wouldn't race for them. I might have enjoyed their company, and we would have a lovely date, but no butterflies ever made an appearance.

My friend Mercedes told me about an independent film called *The Timer* that I watched after our chat. This led to a conversation I had with Apple about how we all know when our timer goes off. It's when our head and heart are in sync with one another. There is no battle of H & H but a formula of H + H = H to the second power. Head and Heart equals harmony, period. Let me expand further on this formula as it leads me to a bible passage that says, ``How can two be equally yoked?'' which the literal interpretation of being equally yoked meaning joined with the same. In agricultural terms the saying goes something like this: if a yoke joins two oxen together, then they need to be the same in order to work together. Hence the formula Head and Heart, the same, as one. They both need to agree, and if not, it's because something is out of balance, not perfectly aligned with our inner soul.

Upon more digging into this formula, I started to realize that there are three categories when you meet someone. The three buckets are these:

- Lust

- Chemistry

- Connection

Lust---we know---is that sexual want, the external part of a human being, a desired entanglement of two bodies.

Chemistry is a feeling of attraction and in that having bits of internal and external magnetic pulls that include desire.

Connection is something that can't be explained. It's the divine meeting of two souls. They don't necessarily have to be your type, and many times they are exactly the opposite of what you envision for yourself. It's a powerful force stronger than lust and chemistry. It's what connects the mind, body, and soul. The triple H is the gift of connection---head and heart blending into harmony.

So, the question now was this: Is my Brazilian Johan my triple H? The answer was more than obvious, it was a hard no. I knew that if my head and heart were not aligned, I would absolutely be settling. All I knew was that his timing was perfect for coming into my life when he did as it was the bridge to bringing my spirit back to life and enjoy the process of dating without the strings attached! We clearly had lust and chemistry, but the connection of our souls was indeed missing.

Chapter 25

BBB

My dating experiences would continue to surprise me in Barcelona. I made no apologies either as I was having fun and not wanting to settle down at this point. A conscious decision I made.

I had met this Catalan man named Alex at a dance club called Sutton while I was out with my girlfriends one night. Later that evening we ended up chatting for hours, and I found him extremely interesting. Now to be fair when I found out he was ten years younger than I was, I wanted to write him off, but the more we spoke the more I was drawn to him. He had a lot of ambition and drive and not to mention was incredibly good looking. He was an engineer and had an incredibly sexy accent. He asked me out on a date; that week we met for drinks. He spoke English, which was a nice breath of air, so I could express myself effortlessly. He lived in San Francisco for a while when he was studying. We talked for hours; it was easy and flowed so naturally. Alex really stimulated my heart which to me was so sexy, and then his eyes, his deep dark brown eyes, would lock into mine, and I would get a quick flutter. At the end of the night, he walked me to a cab, and before I could open the cab door to go home, he went in and kissed me! It was an amazing kiss! I didn't want it to stop, but I had to go. As I drove off in the cab, he texted me right away saying, "What a shame that kiss had to be stopped. I hope it will continue another day. Have a good night, pretty writer." I literally was smiling ear to ear. I liked him. I really liked him, but I didn't let my heart get ahead of myself.

I was leaving for a trip the following week to Freiburg, Germany, to see my good friend Wendy whom I met while we were in Castellano classes the year before here in Barcelona. Alex really wanted to see me again for another date before my trip. I agreed to see him that upcoming weekend. We had such a great first date the week before at the Dow Jones, a place where the drinks change in price like the stock market. I thought to myself, why not? He took me to such a cute place that one of his friends recommended to him. We were outside on the patio sipping some tasty and refreshing tropical drinks while enjoying each other's company. We laughed and always had amazing conversations about everything. I quickly forgot his age; the truth was I didn't care. It was just a number to me now. I loved looking into his eyes; I mean I could stare at him all day. As the night ended, he walked me to the cab again, but before he could wave one down, we started to kiss. I mean really start to kiss, heavily and passionately as my body was feeling all the side effects of this kiss. I wanted him, and I knew he wanted me. He told me he just couldn't let me go home but rather asked me to come back to his apartment. It was nearby, and so without hesitation I agreed to accompany him back to his place. I know that I hold the most incredible honor and role as mom, but that doesn't mean my vagina has to be on lockdown until my son is eighteen.

Alex and I were walking hand in hand towards his home, and he assured me that his brother wouldn't be there. I said, "Oh, you live with your brother?"

He replied, "Yes and I live with my parents as well." Now, you have to understand that in Spain and Catalunya, it is very common that lots of grown adult men still live with their parents. Some even live with their parents up to the age of forty! So to be fair in this case it was typically not a big deal culturally as it would be in the United States, for example. However, I have been living on my own since the age of eighteen, so yes, of course, this bothered me. He then assured me his parents would not be home either as they were at their second home. I willingly overlooked this because all I knew was this: I wanted him, and I wanted him now.

We got to his apartment, or should I say his parent's apartment, and he led me to his bedroom. He opened his bedroom door, and I was in such disbelief! I couldn't believe what was in his room at his age. I never would have guessed! This had to be some kind of joke that Ashton Kutcher was orchestrating for his TV show *Punk'd* or some hidden camera show to capture my near shocked reaction on my face. There it was---a bunk bed, a twin bunk bed with nothing on the bottom because his school desk was there and a ladder to get to the top! Ladies and gentlemen, I suddenly realized I wasn't with Alex but BBB: BUNK BED BOY!

I looked at him and just started laughing! I wanted to run out of there so fast and never look back! I thought to myself, NO! You can do this! This will be the most hilarious sexual experience I could ever have! So, I took a deep breath, unzipped my black high boots, and climbed up that ladder!

Chapter 26

From One Culture to the Next

Jeremiah and I were off to Freiburg, Germany, to spend eight fun filled days with my beautiful friend Wendy and her immediate family members. I always love getting together with her as it makes me reminisce about the two months we spent in Spanish class in Barcelona---the laughs on how much fun we had when we were partnered up by our language instructor. Our friendship was something special I knew would last past the classroom and last a lifetime. Wendy insisted Jeremiah and I experience Fastnacht's! Fastnacht in Germany is like a Carnival or Mardi Gras and let me tell you if you get a chance to go, absolutely go! So many people focus so much on Oktoberfest they don't even know about this fun local party happening in many German cities typically during the month of February! She assured me in the evenings her mom would watch Jeremiah and not to worry that there would be lots to do with him during the day as they had parades and so much more!

The first night we dressed up in white and red high knee striped socks. Wendy had a white bonnet, and I wore a white night cap. Thanks to Wendy for making sure I had the proper attire for the first night's festivities. The men had either a red and white striped shirt or blue and white striped shirt on with matching socks as well. Every night thereafter everyone dressed up in different costumes. The beer, brats, and music kept flowing! I felt like the shiny new toy from America amongst the men. Not to say I didn't love the attention as they were all so attractive! Who knew being single could be so much fun?

As the days went on, Wendy's mom and stepdad took Jeremiah and me to have a slice of Black Forest Cake. Deep in the woods of the Black Forest nestled this little restaurant. This is where we would have Black Forest cake in the Black Forest for our first experience. Cheesy? Yes, but I love it! The mountains were refreshing and a place where gratitude continued to flow within me.

I left Germany with an even deeper appreciation for my German roots. The only problem now is I couldn't get the song Fliegerlied mit, with the words "Flieg, Flieg, schwimm, schwimm, La la la la!" still lingering and replaying in my head for weeks thereafter! I knew I would be back again to my great grandparents' home country.

The following month it was time to head out to incredible Istanbul. I couldn't wait to board my Turkish Airline plane while sitting at the Barcelona airport and get Apple's thirtieth birthday bash of festivities started! On the plane in route to Istanbul, I am soaring through the deep blue sky, and the sun starts to gently shine on my face and across these very pages that I am writing on. I look below and see the sun's reflection on the Bosphorus waters. God's beauty, His work of art, is all around me. Suddenly the universe starts to whisper in my ear, "Embrace the moment." So, I do.

Istanbul has been a destination that has been on my wish list and my vision board, and now that is coming to fruition, someone just pinch me! I can't even contain my excitement! I have said it often, and I will say it again: I truly have a love affair with travel, a soul full of wanderlust and a travel bug spirit! Whenever Apple and I get together, it is always a guaranteed time of fun surely to be filled with unforgettable experiences. Wherever it is in the world that you want to explore and travel, begin with a clear vision and set your mind. Know that you are going, not hope, not maybe, but ARE. Speak it into existence, in the present tense, and say, "I am going to…...!" It's another reason I believe in the power of a vision board that it should be the first thing you see daily. When you can mentally see and feel what you want, where you want to go the universe will conspire to make it happen and give you clues to the tools in order to take action that will give you those very results. The more real the feeling you have, the higher that vibration of frequency will go out into the universe. Trust me the doors of the universe will guide you to a path to make it happen. We often want guarantees and how it will happen. You have to simply know it will happen and follow the breadcrumbs that will lead you to whatever city, country, and/or dream you may have in life. I am living proof it works! The Law of Attraction is proof that you are a walking magnet of your thoughts. It is so easy for many of us to limit ourselves, and, therefore, you are the one who cheats yourself out of a dream that is attainable. I did it for so long, too long! All my dreams were attainable, and I truly believe in what Winston Churchill said, "What the mind can see the mind can achieve."

Disembarking the plane in Istanbul, I walk towards the nearest ATM as I always do when I travel to withdraw local currency. This time it was a different experience. Suddenly, the machine ran out of money and still debited my bank account the amount I requested! What??? A man with a British accent approached me and said, "You need to use the other ATM as this just happened to me, too!" I had never had this happen in all my travels. Thank God, I had another card on me to withdraw money from another ATM machine. A couple of lessons I learned is to always say yes you want a receipt so when you go to dispute it with your bank you have proof. I also realized that having more than one debit or credit card on me was essential should an emergency such as this situation ever occur again.

Apple was at our private hostel as I was on my way learning a few new Turkish words from my taxi driver. I freshened up, and the two of us were ready to light the streets of Istanbul! Two beautiful single women were amongst some very handsome Turkish men. This trip was one of the first moments in my life where I realized I had truly made a shift in myself. What I mean is that I always smile, and I think most people would say that I am a sweet, kind, funny, and pretty much the life of the party type of gal. Since living in Barcelona, I have dated a lot with a very different mindset than I ever had. The cultural difference gave me a different grasp simply because it truly was a completely different way of dating. You've got to be tough, or the men will eat you alive with their sweetness and with one mission and one mission only: Get into your goody bag!

Of course, I am not saying that is a bad thing either if that is all you are looking for. That is A-Okay! I mean I did with BBB because I wasn't looking for anything more. If you have zero expectations, practice safe sex, and, of course, if you stop yourself from planning your wedding as soon as you lock eyes well, then by all means have fun and again have safe fun! I am also not saying all men are like this either, but you have got to really weed them out.

So, for me at least Barcelona has made me tougher in the sense that it got me out of fairytale land, that fantasy land really quick! Apple, having noticed my demeanor and having experienced the dating scene herself, yanks my arm and says to me, "Annie! Annie! We aren't in Barcelona anymore. You don't have to be so tough. He is trying!" I have to be honest. It was refreshing because I didn't want to be so tough almost to the point of a bitch when it was not even necessary. I immediately snapped out of it, and in doing so we started to have a blast amongst the locals. For the record, the Turkish people are some of the nicest I have ever encountered. The following evening, I met Oskar, a very handsome beautiful green-eyed Turkish man at a supper club that was filled with great energy and vibes! He only spoke a few words in English, and I only knew a handful of Turkish words, but we had an instant attraction. I realized "love" or "attraction" has only one language, and we all speak it. I mean my parents met and my mom spoke no Spanish and my dad knew very little English when he came to America in his twenties, but six weeks later they got married and have been married for over forty-five years! Sometimes it just works out that way. Now for the record I was not in love or smitten with Oskar but attracted and interested in him. Our conversations were best defined in the form of kissing throughout the night. It was easy to see how I got the nickname kissing bandit as it was seemingly becoming my favorite activity. I wasn't sure if we would ever meet again, but the one thing I can be sure of is how he played such a memorable part in my Turkish experience. Like a gentleman he and his friend walked Apple and me back to our hostile in the early hours of the morning. Apple was not in the very least interested or attracted to Oskar's friend, but she was the best wing woman I could ever ask for! With a last kiss goodbye, Oskar and I exchanged numbers and kept in touch.

Apple had met this beautiful Persian, Iranian beauty named Mary at our hostel the day before I arrived. She would join us on some of our adventures here in Istanbul. I was very intrigued by Mary's stories of being a woman living in the Middle East. It was a lovely Saturday afternoon, and the three of us set out to have lunch. The three of us in our thirties were from all different parts of the world---me from the United States of America, Apple from the Philippines, and Mary from Iran. We sat there exchanging stories and comparing the differences in each of our cultures as women. It was mind blowing! I didn't realize this would be one of the richest lunches of my life! I also was never more grateful to be an American than at that moment and have the sincerest form of gratitude for my freedom and all the men and women who have died for that privilege. I can't say thank you enough. Another eye opener is how so many of us around the world live in a bubble and make assumptions. This is why travel is so important. You become slightly less ignorant. Mary taught me more in one afternoon than any news outlet could teach. She taught me more about the Quran and how so many misinterpret it. I can't even express how grateful I am that her path crossed ours. I am so grateful for her sharing and teaching me about her culture.

We decided we would head off to the blue mosque. When we arrived, this would be my first experience putting a hijab and covering my hair. My friend Mary took my blue hijab and wrapped it properly for me. I indulged every second of this moment knowing I am walking in the shoes of what she has to do on the daily in her own country in Iran. I do my best to immerse myself in the culture of any country I visit. In this particular mosque, a hijab was not mandatory to wear so Mary opted out. I can't imagine how it must have felt for her to feel a sense of liberation, choice if you will, and not to mention she had gorgeous long black silky locks of hair. Mary is here in Turkey because she fell in love with a Turkish man, but soon he will move to Canada, and she will have an opportunity to live with him in Canada which makes her beyond ecstatic! Mary has been such a great addition to all the strong and beautiful women I have met from all around the world. To complete my trip here in Istanbul, I recruited Apple to join me in assisting with finding me the perfect meditation carpet to take home with me. Ah, there it was after what seemed as an endless search---my meditation carpet that felt as if it was made just for me. I was so excited like a kid in a candy store! I made Apple take a picture of me holding it!

I truly fell in love with this beautiful city! The gratitude I have for Istanbul's warm and loving arms opening to me will forever be embedded in my mind!

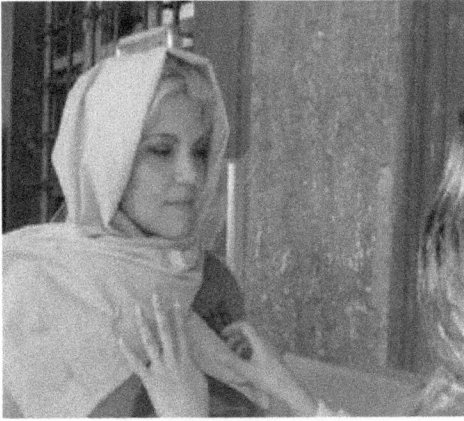

My beautiful friend from Iran, Mary, properly wraps on my sky-blue hijab before I enter the Blue Mosque.

Chapter 27

Summer Travels

It was my third scorching hot summer in Barcelona, and I couldn't imagine living anywhere else in the world! My body was now accumulated to the scorching Spanish hot sun, yummy tapas, and sandy beaches, and all I could feel was a sense of home.

I was moving out of my current apartment in Gràcia which proved to be an insane nightmare to say the least. I could write a book on it called "When Landlords Are Crooks." However, I was not going to let this mishap ruin my summer adventure. My twelve-year-old Jeremiah was all packed up and off to see his father for another summer. Watching Jeremiah leave at the airport and going through security every summer never got easier for me. I always felt a piece of me missing as I would stand there at the airport and have one more last glance as he headed through security. Gosh, I was going to miss my boy tremendously!

I ended the school year teaching at the English academy but still continued with my private English tutoring for extra income. One of my students close in age to me, Paulo, was an architect wanting to improve his English. I met Paulo through his ex-boyfriend as I was private tutoring his niece Chelsey. Paulo and I would always meet in a nearby local coffee shop and practice. He was a joy to be around, and the laughs were always endless when we would meet. He was a true world traveler, and his next adventure was going to be moving to South Africa. This meant that his apartment here in Barcelona was going to be available in September. What perfect timing! "I'll take it!" I said. He was so happy to have someone he trusted that would be living there, and he had all the comfort in knowing that I would take care of it. He wouldn't even accept a security deposit from me. I was excited that I would soon be back in my old neighborhood of Poble Sec come the Fall. In the meantime, until then, I would live with Apple and her roommates through the summer months of June through August. Summer nights in Barcelona are simply put filled with life! The place to be where my friends and I would spend countless nights at Mac Arena Mar which was a Beach Club with all the Ibiza vibes! International DJs would set the tone as we danced away on the sandy beach until the wee hours of the morning! Opposite of the DJ stage was the Mediterranean Sea splashing back to the musical sounds. Some of my best summer memories were filled with Apple, Robin, and the guys whom I met through Robin. One of them, in particular, Darcio, the one with the blue rimmed sunglasses, had this contagious energy and smile that you just couldn't help but always feel good around him! If you are having a bad day, just turn around and watch Darcio over in the sand dancing his butt away, waving his arm in the air to the beats with an endless smile! I loved his energy! Seriously, any guy would be lucky to have him!

I always was very conscientious about remaining present in the moment. Allowing gratitude to flow endlessly. I did this often whether I was at the beach or just walking down the street in

Barcelona, I would take it all in and give thanks to God and the universe for blessing me in creating this beautiful life. I was ready to start my thirty-fifth birthday trip to Ireland and Scotland with Apple. We rented a car, and I gladly volunteered not to drive! I mean the driver's seat is on the opposite side than the cars in America. The roads are opposite, and with my track record of car accidents it probably was best to give the coveted role to Apple. She was confident with her driving skills, so we decided we would start in Dublin and go north along the coast until we reached the city of Cork. We could have continued on through Wicklow and ended back in Dublin, but I wanted to ensure we didn't enter the Wicklow area which is known as the garden of Ireland. I had made a promise to my son Jeremiah that we would do that trip together. We both loved the movie *P.S. I Love You* so that was on our future mom and son bucket list trip.

In Dublin, we stayed at Kelly's place. She was from San Diego and met Apple one day when she was vacationing in Barcelona while in line ordering tapas. It was so great getting to get to know Kelly and have her show us all around. She introduced me to my first Iced Frappuccino. Yes, my first! Boy, did I fall in love with it. It gave me intense energy even when this energizer bunny didn't need any more! I always enjoyed the Pride Festival in Chicago, but this would be my first International Pride Fest in Dublin. I loved seeing everyone celebrating that LOVE IS LOVE!

This was my third time in Dublin, but the first time that I finally got to see in person The Book of Kells at the Trinity College Library. It looked like a scene from Harry Potter. Was I suddenly in Hogwarts?

After a few days we left Kelly's apartment to continue our Ireland adventure. Kelly would join us again when Apple and I would be in the latter portion of our trip in Edinburgh, Scotland.

Driving up north towards Belfast we had to see for ourselves the famous UNESCO (United Nations Educational, Scientific and Cultural Organization) World Heritage site New Grange Monument. These prehistoric Irish passage tombs date all the way back to 3200 BC which are older than Stonehenge and the Egyptian pyramids! We left quite impressed to say the least. We then decided to go a little off course and make a pit stop in the cozy town of Carlingford. This city turned out to be a little unexpected gem that detoured our route but only for the better! We stopped at King John's Castle that was from the 12th century. Enjoying our day, we continued to walk a bit further only to discover there was a Viking festival happening on the streets. A table filled with a Viking food spread set the tone as if we went back in time. There stood a handful of men in their Viking attire and war paint. We smiled and observed as we carried on allowing our roaring hungry tummies to lead the way! PJ's Oyster Bar and Restaurant seemed so lively as you could hear the live band playing outdoors. Their menu also offered an array of food with a great atmosphere. We thought why not try it here! Browsing through the menu, I noticed chicken kiev, which always reminded me of my childhood with Yana. I decided my pallet was saying go for it! The waitress brought our dishes, and to say I had the most delicious chicken kiev of my life, possibly in the world, would be an understatement! It was juicy and savory, and with every bite my taste buds were applauding! We quickly were forewarned of the fifty-thousand-euro reward to the person who finds the missing leprechaun from their poster that was hung up! Apple and I chuckled at it. We surely enjoyed this seaside town, but it was time to head off to our next and final stop for the evening!

Arriving in Belfast where the currency had now changed to the UK's pound, we headed to our private hostel for a good night sleep. Ready to go bright and early the next day, we met our tour guide and taxi driver along with a handful of us ready to experience the Black Taxi Tour of Belfast. We had an old vintage red car there waiting for us. In the back seat was Apple, a blonde girl from Australia named Analise, and me. We were looking forward to our Political and Mural tour. Belfast had been through so much during their civil war which ended with the Good Friday Agreement of 1998. I remember as a teenager watching on the news the battle between the Protestants and Catholics from my living room in America. I remember feeling such sadness for the children who had to walk to school in fear in the midst of so much danger. The taxi drivers of this company are from both sides Catholic and Protestant and personally lived through the bloodshed. Our personal taxi driver was able to really transport us back in time as to what it was like. The peace wall had everyone from around the world with different quotes of peace but one that stood out to us: "Peace starts with a BBQ and VB. Come to Australia" My new made friend Analise confirmed the quote with a laugh! "What's a VB?" I said. Analise, replied "A Lager Beer". That made a ton of sense to Apple and me! Hmm, I liked the Australian way of thinking! We then began to contribute our own peace quote with the marker given to us and write on the wall.

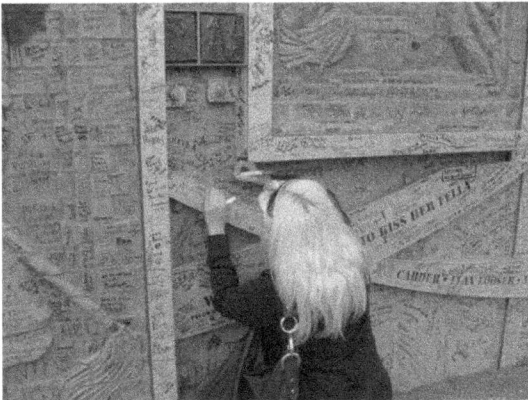

Signing the Peace Wall in Belfast.

Apple, Analise, and I then decided to head for a cold beer after our tour. The Crown Liquor Saloon which dates back to the 1880s has amazing architectural details made with etched glass, carved mahogany booths, and glass lamps that really make this place stand out. We got to know Analise more and loved that she was a strong and independent woman from the LGBT community traveling solo. She was hilarious and tons of fun! We toasted and made sure we would always keep in touch.

The following day we headed more north and drove to the Carrick-a-rede bridge where these views were just absolutely picturesque! The rope bridge is not for the faint at heart as it spans ninety-eight feet high and sixty-six feet in length! Of course, we had to experience walking across this shaky bridge! Apple recorded the sounds of the wind, and our shoes swayed on the bridge as we looked down to see how high we were. We truly enjoyed it!

Then it was off to the only UNESCO World Heritage Site in Northern Ireland, The Giant Causeway. This is truly a unique site to see as the hexagonal columns are all a result of an ancient volcanic fissure eruption. It is absolutely an incredible beauty, and to have it only magnified by the coastline creates one extraordinary backdrop! The whole coast of Northern Ireland looked like a post card. It didn't even look real. It was simply so stunning---God's art on every corner!

We were headed to the Northwest and decided to rest in Donegal. We saw what looked like a bed and breakfast and politely knocked on the door to see if there was availability. It was late at night, so we were grateful for the hospitality that was showed. "Yes, we have space." She replied. The next day we woke up and were wowed by the beauty here in Donegal! There was so much nature, and you could find cows and sheep everywhere! I have a major obsession with sheep! I have this vision where I just want to be in the middle of a ton of them like a shepherd! Apple would just give me a look of here goes another one of Annie's crazy ideas again! "Leave the sheep alone!", said Apple as we both just laugh!

Next was the town of Sligo. Since leaving Dublin almost a week ago, I was on a quest the past several days to find a cup of Iced Frappuccino that was as delicious as the one I had back in Dublin. The winner: SLIGO!!! A coffee bar called Costa was found. Our barista was a young woman with short blond hair who thoroughly enjoyed my excitement when she saw my reaction to their menu. "I have been looking everywhere! We will each have a large Iced Frappuccino please!" She gladly whipped them up for us. I asked if

I could take a picture of her to remember my mission for my new beloved iced Frappuccino. She posed with a big smile while holding up both of them in the air. She was my hero for the day! I mean it's the little things in life to be grateful for. We merrily went on our way and headed into the heart of this charming town. We began to take a stroll and have a yummy vegetarian lunch before we would leave to the city of Galway. Galway was a lively town where we got to enjoy tons of live music, many shops, Atlantic coastline, and more! It was also home to where the first Claddagh ring was made. Of course, I had to get one since I lost my last one. I loved how the symbols had different meanings. The hands represent friendship, the heart symbolizes true love, and the crown is for loyalty. You wear it on your right hand, and if the crown is turned outwards and away from you, it indicates that you are single. To wear the Claddagh ring with the crown turned inward and towards you symbolizes that someone has your heart or that you are in a relationship. I took my stainless-steel Claddagh ring and wore it with the crown away from me showing that I was very much single!

We continued to see the Dunguaire Castle and then to the

famous Cliffs of Moher. These cliffs were beauties and definitely a must see! We decided to take a short cut for time's sake and cross the ferry with our rental car from the gorgeous landscape of the Dingle Peninsula to head where we would make a pit stop for some shopping and dinner in Killarney. Truthfully, when we arrived, I wished we had more time so we could have stayed longer. There was a charm I loved in Killarney. We headed off to our final city for a couple of nights in Cork. Cork was absolutely one of my most favorite cities in Ireland! I loved the energy of this place. The people were just so friendly, and the town was so quaint. It wasn't long until we made other friends and enjoyed the nightlife here. It was a great way to end Ireland. We stayed at a fun hostel where we met some amazing people from other parts of the globe. It was time to fly to Edinburgh, Scotland, and meet up with Kelly again! It was all our first time in this city, so we couldn't wait to check into our charming apartment situated on Rosebery Crescent Lane. I quickly unpacked my suitcase and placed my framed picture of Jeremiah and I on the nightstand next to my bed.

I was in my final days of being thirty-four years old. As I

reflected on just how much I loved this decade in my thirties thus far, the person I have become doesn't even look remotely close to the woman I was in my twenties. I would not even recognize her now.

We had dinner at a nearby Chinese restaurant and went out with no plans on where to go. We quickly walked down a street where we saw red lights and decided to check it out. Lulu's was absolutely buzzing and had a ton of young men in kilts. I mean who doesn't love a man in a kilt? I loved that I could feel the Scottish heritage amongst us.

Our next full day we went to the Edinburgh Castle where an ice cream truck named Asher's was there. I personally have ice cream every blue moon, and boy, was I glad I decided to join my friends for some. It was beyond delicious---creamy and perfect! We kept walking toward the Edinburgh Castle where there were guards yet again in kilts---two, in particular, with very serious faces guarding the outside. I went up to them both and asked, "Is it true what they say about there being nothing else to wear under one man's kilt?" They both couldn't help but start to laugh! Breaking out of character, they both took a picture with me smiling---one with an even bigger smile as he placed his white gloved left hand around my shoulder ready for our pic. I loved that in the midst of being serious they were able to lighten up and have some fun!

We continued down the cobble stone streets in town and observed our atmosphere. There were plenty of bag pipers playing. One, in particular, was dressed as half man and half animal as the lower part of his body was in animal skins and his feet were in hooves. I glanced across and saw a businessman with his briefcase, white collar shirt, tie, and green kilt rushing down the street. I was embracing all of this!

We went into a bar to try a scotch. I told the bartender if he could recommend a scotch and please on ice. The bartender said, "On ice?"

"Yes", I replied. He proceeded to tell me a good scotch doesn't need any ice and should be neat. I was up for the challenge!

"One scotch neat please." He poured me a Glenkinchie 12.

My first sip sang! It was smooth and exceeded my expectations. "No more ice!" I said as he smiled.

The following day it was my thirty-fifth birthday! I decided to wear a sky-blue one shoulder dress I bought in town the other day. I love Indian food, and Scotland was known to have some amazing ones. We had reservations at Omar Khaggam - No. 1 Finest Indian and Punjabi Cuisine. The three of us ordered a bottle of red wine and an array of Indian food which included garlic naan that was as big as two people's head! Then came out a huge slice of chocolate birthday cake with a 3 and 5 candle ready for me to blow and make a wish. This was the perfect birthday dinner! The food was so delicious that I so look forward to going back there.

We would end the night dancing away and go into the early morning playing cards and slot machines at a nearby casino. Kelly had to fly back to Dublin, and Apple and I still had a full day ahead of us. We found a park filled with people. We rested on the green grass and basked in the sun enjoying the weather. We ended the day by going to the Palace of Holyroodhouse, the Queen's Official Residence in Scotland. What a whirlwind of a trip filled with all the ingredients I could ever ask for!

When I asked Apple years later what were some of her fondest memories she said, "I think Ireland. We went there to celebrate your birthday, and since you loved Ireland so much, the enthusiasm was infectious. We spent a lot of time together *(not that we didn't before that... hahaha)* but we also had a lot of crazy adventures. The people were friendly although a bit shy which was super strange for us coming from Spain. Like night and day! I say it's memorable, too, because there were mostly just the two of us, and I like that. We can focus on each other and experience everything the way we both want it. You are one of the best travel buddies because we *mostly* like the same things, and even if we didn't, we are both laid back enough just to enjoy it. Sitting here, memories are flooding in, and I just remember your obsession with taking a pic with a sheep to the point we kept stopping on the side of the road and you thinking of ways to jump the fence or the fact we even bothered a man outside his home and asked him if we could go to his field so you can take a picture! Annie, you always seem to have a goal in each trip, like for example, in Istanbul you wanted to have a rug, where even though you couldn't afford an original Turkish rug, a Chinese made one will do. But hey! You bought it in Turkey! You always have a vision of the experience you would like to have, and I admire you for it."

I loved that I got to relive Apple's version which is absolutely spot on!

Days later after Apple and I returned from Scotland, we found ourselves yet again repacking our bags and off to Pamplona, the famous Running of the Bulls! We took a six-hour bus ride from Barcelona. Apple's roommate was from Pamplona, so she was so gracious to let a handful of other friends and us stay as guests at her parents' home. This is a festival that should come with a warning label: NO SLEEP! The party does not stop, and the streets are flooded with so many people from around the world all wearing the same two colors, white and red! It's a beautiful sight of the world all coming together and having one huge party!

In the midst of the crowd, I also was able to meet up from my Peruvian friend Ada whom I met in a photograph class in

Barcelona. There she would be introduced to Apple. The several days we were there seemed like one long sleepless night blended into one---one of the most incredible festivals I have ever experienced!

The last day was the actual Running of the Bulls. I was so naive as the thought of this amazing gathering could end with such cruelty to these innocent animals. Apple and I were in the stands sobbing. We couldn't bear to watch them antagonize these beautiful creatures. It wasn't right. How could I be so ignorant not to know what happened at this festival? We had to leave the stands as tears were streaming down our face. I vowed I would never step foot in another arena again where such cruel activity was being cheered on. How I wish the festival that was so much fun ended in a much different way than this.

Running of the Bulls festival in Pamplona on the streets celebrating with what seems like millions!

There are many times when I close my eyes and remember that little girl who didn't have a lot growing up and daydreaming of traveling the way I am now. I am so grateful for The Law of Attraction teachings that showed me the way to reset and retrain my mindset and manifest all my dreams with no limitations! If I wanted to see the world, I could! It was me holding me back from thinking it wasn't possible for someone like me---a poor kid from Chicago with BIG dreams!

I was back in Barcelona later that month in July. Apple headed to her vanity table to get ready for the day as I sat on her bed getting ready to Skype with Jeremiah. I always had so much anticipation before he would come on video. I missed him so, so, so much! "Jeremiah! I miss you so much!", I shouted. We began to chat, but suddenly this conversation wasn't like any other conversation we ever had on our Skype calls.

Jeremiah started to express passionately how much he missed being in America. He expressed how much he missed all his friends back home. He was agonizing over the thought of coming back for a third year to Barcelona. He started to cry profusely.

Seeing him so sad and what almost seemed like a plea of desperation for me not to make him go back made my heart sink. Holding my tears back as best as I could, I told him not to worry that I would be back in America soon as I always was in August, and we would discuss it further.

What Jeremiah didn't know was that in that very second, I knew I was going back to America. I needed Jeremiah to know he was being heard and his feelings mattered.

I closed my laptop after our chat, and without any thought or hesitation I looked over to Apple and said, "I am going back to America." Her shocked and devastated countenance was only a reflection of what mine was only seconds ago as I was just in the midst of having finalized my plans for year three here. "Apple, there is no way I can make Jeremiah come back if he is this miserable. I want him to be happy. I know I can always come back here and make Barcelona my home again when he goes to college." I knew in my heart to stay would be the most selfish thing; my number one priority and love of my life is and will always be my son. It was the right thing to do.

Apple replied with complete understanding. Then stated, "Should I leave now, too? Should I go to Paris for a while?" And so on as we both laughed with unknown futures ahead of us!

Chapter 28

Adios!

The hardest part about leaving Barcelona was going to be saying goodbye to all these lifelong friendships I have made.

As the news suddenly spread to all my friends including my students, there was a somberness. Nevertheless, there was a sense of it being quite bittersweet leaving on such a high note with the memories made. I knew the excitement when I would tell my son we weren't coming back to Barcelona would mean everything to him and that his voice was being heard. Since Jeremiah was a little child, I would repeatedly tell him, "You have a voice. It doesn't matter how old you are, and never let anyone make you feel that you don't." I truly believe every child's voice matters.

Every August in my old neighborhood of Gràcia, there is an annual festival where the district shows off their decorating skills and fills each street with decorations! Each street has its own theme and decorates with such vastly unique creativity. If only Salvador Dali was still alive to see these creative minds at work. Recyclable materials, plastic bottles, and paper are used to transport these streets to life. This festival is a main attraction to locals and tourist!

Typically, you could always find me back in Chicago during the month of August visiting my friends and family but not today, not this August. I decided to extend my stay since I was leaving indefinitely now. This was going to be my very first experience at the Gràcia Festival which is also known as Les Festes de Gràcia. Apple and I first had to stop for dinner at one our favorite Italian restaurants called Pappa E Citti. This gem of a restaurant always transported me to Italy every time. The red wine from Sicily just welcomes your pallet with each bite of pasta you take. The owners are so warm and welcoming which simply puts this place in a category of its own. It surely doesn't disappoint!

We left with filled bellies ready to experience the festival. The bustling streets were filled with people all in awe of the work that was put in street after street, block after block. I quickly could see why this summer festival was a highlight in Barcelona.

My time felt as if it was on an hourglass sand timer almost out. Apple and I would fill many nights out in town or on the beach for another last hurrah. On one of our last evenings out on the beach I met a handsome blue-eyed Italian who was visiting Barcelona. He was keen on getting to know me and I thought why not? I invited him to come to my big going away party that was happening that weekend. He gladly accepted and said he would be there.

I had a notebook that I wanted to make sure that every one of my friends would sign in and write a goodbye note or memory we shared so I could read it on the plane ride home and have as a keepsake. I had this idea when I was leaving the United States to come here to Barcelona. It was as if I had a piece of my friends with me on my new journey. Every gathering from here on out I ensured my notebook was with me.

It was only appropriate to have my going away party at my regular hang out Gato Negro in Gràcia where my friends La Reina, Oscar, and Olen aka Smiley worked at. They reserved a long table in the back that had a cold, bubbly bottle of cava waiting for us on ice that we would use to toast with. One by one my friends arrived including my blue eyed Italian. He sat to the left of me with a drink in hand ready to celebrate with all my friends. To the right of me was Katie, my very first friend I made here. Next to Katie there sat my two Bostonian friends who lived abroad in Australia for quite some time. Next to them was Carl who was one of Apple's roommates and made the best nachos a girl could ever ask for! Directly across from me sat Robin and Apple who both were still trying to wrap their mind that I was actually leaving the Three Musketeers. On Apple's right side sat my British mate Derrick and his wife, my good friend Carlota. I met them through Lucas's friend's friend, and we never let our breakup disturb our continued friendship. Carlota had a son who was the same age as Jeremiah. I was so grateful that we would have our sons come together to begin a friendship. They gave me the sweetest card with a Barcelona gastronomy and cuisine cookbook. This foodie couldn't have asked for a better gift! Through Derrick and Carlota, we met our two other friends Mario and his girlfriend. Last but not least was my brother from another mother, Joseph, and another friend I met through him, Franco. Julian and Monte, Joseph's brother, were not in the country at that time, but they were there in spirit. The drinks were coming, and Joseph did the honors to pop that bubbly of cava so all my friends could toast to the amazing memories! My notebook was going around with everyone making sure to write their goodbyes. We then left and headed to the same night club where we celebrated on New Year's. We laughed, drank, and danced the night away! Round one of the goodbyes were complete and so was round one with my blue eyed Italian. Unfortunately, I just didn't feel a connection. I was grateful to have met him and have his friendship.

Later that week I would meet with Mercedes, my beautiful friend that I met the same night that I met Apple. We went shopping where I bought a black and white canvas of Barcelona to take back home with me. We went and sat down to have lunch, and Mercedes gifted me with a smaller canvas of a Vespa, scooter that I saw and loved; a light peach and coral scarf; and finally, a butterfly magnet.

She told me the butterfly is a symbol of my growth and how I was ready to fly. I smiled and cried while hugging her hoping she would now the gravity of how much her friendship has meant to me here in Barcelona.

As the weekend suddenly was approaching Katie and her boyfriend wanted to throw a smaller going away party for me with a handful of friends in her home. "Katie, please make your delicious taco salad dip.", I said with the biggest grin.

The day of the gathering had arrived, and it was the perfect blend of intimacy amongst close friends. Katie made her yummy taco salad dip, an array of Spanish cheeses, meats, and olives took center stage. There was, of course, bottles and bottles of delicious red Spanish wine to accommodate our pallets through the night.

There was a total of seven of us which included Apple, Robin, and my two Bostonian friends. We reminisced, laughed, drank, and ate to our hearts' content. The six of them decided they would record a video for me. It goes something like this:

"Annie, please don't leave! Come back!!!!!!!!" They

shouted with so much passion!

Holding my tears back and taking a deep breath to the incredible life I had made here in the last two plus years, I was consumed with joy.

Another week of goodbyes would start with my dear friend Larissa. How was I going to hold back the tears? Larissa and her family had played a big part in my experience here. We met for a delicious lunch that she kindly treated me to. Memories of how we first met at Gato Negro to where our friendship was today only made us grateful for having our paths cross when they did. We headed down to the beach for drinks at a chringuito, called Del Sol, where Smiley also worked at besides Gato Negro. I squeezed these two so hard and knew I would see them in the near future again.

The following day I met with the gorgeous Robin and my lovely friend Lionel. I loved getting to know him at our beach parties over the past summers here. I was grateful Robin introduced us. We met up at La Xampanyeria, a bustling tapas bar that mirrored the Wall Street stock exchange, chaotic, noisy, yet so exciting! This was the place to get proper tapas! Standing and ordering with endless glasses of cava at fifty cents each that kept coming, I couldn't believe I never was here before!

Glancing over at Robin I was flooded with our priceless memories! How hilarious she was when it came to men. Their teeth were either too big, their lips too small, not beardy enough, and the list goes on. I was truly going to miss meeting her for our chats and wine. I most definitely was going to miss her infectious laugh! Calling dibs when we were attracted to the same guy. Saying goodbye to one of my best mates was proving to be tougher than I can ever expect.

I was continuing my rounds of goodbyes. Meeting my Turkish queen AJ, I was flooded with the memory of how with just her champagne glassed cava garnished with a fresh strawberry started our friendship and how she was our connection in meeting Robin. We ordered a plate of delicious grilled zucchini topped with goat cheese, chatted, hugged, and said our goodbyes as she wrote her final words in my little notebook. Things started to really become real that I was leaving the city I have grown to love.

Paulo and I would have our last goodbye before I took off to Chicago and he to South Africa. I had enjoyed tutoring my architect student but especially getting to know him. He was worldly and funny and spoke English so lovely in his Spanish accent. We met quite often near the English Academy I taught at. Cachitos cafe was a quaint cafe where we would do our English lessons but also learn so much about each other in the process, so it only made sense to have our last meeting there. "Paulo, one day I will come visit you in South Africa," I said. Surely, I'd see him again but until then, I would follow his journey on social media.

It started feeling like a marathon saying my goodbyes to everyone. I wanted to ensure I made time to see everyone before my time here in Barcelona ended. These weeks of goodbyes reminded me of how excited I was just a couple of years back when I was leaving Chicago to come and live here in Barcelona.

Next, I was on my way to Chelsey's apartment in the Sangrada neighborhood. Chelsey was Paulo's ex-boyfriend's niece whom I tutored since she was six to eight years old. Chelsy's mother Magdalena invited me over for dinner. The dinner setting was absolutely so lovely! Bottles of Spanish red wine kept coming as soon as the Gazpecho was served. Then the FISH! Internally, I was saying something like this: "No, no, oh God, no! Oh God, what am I going to do?"

Knowing there is no way after all the trouble that went into preparing this could I say the words:

I DON'T EAT FISH.

I am scared of how it looks, smells, the texture, and all! I don't even eat meat that has bones in it because I will think about the animal. So, the very thought of it touching my pallet was starting to make me feel nauseous.

There was no way I was going to be rude. Annie, think……. okay, I have red wine! I would use the red wine as an anchor. It would be like a red river gushing through my tastebuds cancelling out any fishy taste. I made sure to swallow each piece and not chew every bite. I ultimately survived without Magdalena never knowing that I don't eat fish.

I should always advise what I can't eat before any invitation. It was truly my fault. In the end I was so grateful for Magdalena's invitation and amazing hospitality. It was truly the first time I had gotten to know Magdalena on a whole other level. We both thought why didn't we start hanging out before? We decided to meet at a nearby cafe for our last time to say our goodbyes.

This goodbye was particularly hard with Chelsey. She had been my student for the past two years, and we had gotten very close.

She was a firecracker!

One day when I stepped away in the middle of our English lesson to use the washroom, I accidentally forgot to lock the door. While I was sitting on the toilet, suddenly Chelsey bursts into the washroom and says, "You are using the bathroom? Do you have caca?" I burst out in laughter and gently said to her no I don't and please close the door. Kids say and do the most hilarious things! Chelsey was no exception. She made teaching beyond fun and so memorable!

Chapter 29

Full Circle

I still couldn't believe I was really leaving Barcelona! I quickly realized I really couldn't leave Barcelona without saying a final goodbye to Lucas.

I decided to reach out to Lucas and message him that I was moving back to Chicago and that I was really sad about it but undoubtedly happy for Jeremiah. I told him how he was one of the many reasons why I came and that he was and will always be a very important and special person in my life and heart.

I knew there were no bad feelings but also knew it could feel awkward for us to see each other after so much time had passed. I insisted he didn't feel any pressure, but it would be nice perhaps to get together for a drink and catch up. Lucas responded to first tell me he stopped at Jeremiah's old school, and there was an end of the year party. Lucas didn't know that I put Jeremiah in a private school the following year. He told me how all the students, moreover all the girls, wanted to know where Jeremiah was. Lucas said, "I didn't realize the star he was, and he still is here." Lucas also had let me know that his contract in research had ended, and he had a job back in Paris, France, and was leaving as well. He then proceeded to say that if I am sad because I am leaving Catalunya, then it means that it has been a great time then. I could not have agreed more to his statement.

Lucas agreed he would like to see me for a drink. He also admittedly said that he felt still a tad strange but moreover would be sad if we didn't have a chance to say goodbye. One thing that was for sure for the both of us is that we wanted to return to Barcelona in our near future.

The day had come when I was meeting Lucas. It had been over a year since I had seen him! However, I felt a hundred percent confident that I was absolutely over him. Still tucking away my nervousness, I was so content that I was going to be seeing Lucas face to face. I recommended we meet at one of my favorite restaurants Cerveseria Catalana. He loved that it was somewhere new. It seemed as if I was now the one showing him other parts of Barcelona and not the other way around as when I first arrived as a non-seasoned resident.

The moment we saw each other we both couldn't help but have huge smiles across our countenance as we hugged each other tightly. We sat outside and started with some red Spanish wine and yummy out of this world tapas. "I love this place!" I said, secretly, thinking he would, too. We were both in quite disbelief that we were actually here together. It also felt as if no time had passed, but yet so much had happened since our breakup. I also wasn't the same person anymore. I had simply become unapologetic for being so free here in Barcelona living my life without any judgement.

Hours and hours went by, and we both didn't want the night to end. So we decided to have a cocktail nearby and continue catching up. It now was getting considerably late, and it was a good idea to head home. When we got outside of the cocktail bar, we started to quarrel over something so minute and then without warning he just grabbed me, pulled me in, and kissed me deeply and passionately! There on the main street the atmosphere filled with electrifying heat between our bodies which was seemingly getting more and more intense as the seconds passed by. All the feelings for one another started rushing back in that long passionate kiss. We headed back to my place where Lucas made love to me in one of the most intense, heated, steamiest ways. I was in ecstasy craving each second of his body, his lips, his eyes. The way we looked at each other when we made love was another form of love making. No man had ever made love to me the way Lucas did.

When we woke up, it wasn't strange; it was beautiful, and so we made love again. I took control, pressing my body on top of his while both of our deep brown eyes locked; we just would not let go of one another. Thereafter, lying in his arms I could feel our love had never gone away. We still cared deeply for one another. I kissed him as I walked him to the door. I raced to the window waving goodbye to him knowing that would be our last time together. I felt wonderful for our ending. I wasn't thinking we were getting back together but rather that it was a closure on our love. I let it be and not like the old Annie thinking we are getting back together or that things with us would change. I truly was happy with our ending.

A couple of days had passed, and Lucas hadn't heard from me, so he decided to reach out and send me a message. I was so surprised to say the least. I think he was surprised I didn't reach out to him after our passionate and eventful evening and morning. He wrote that he would like to see me again, one last time before I leave and since I only had two days left. He asked if he could see me today for a coffee. "What time?" I responded.

He said, "Nine, nine thirty p.m.?"

I quickly responded, "Looks like we aren't having coffee but mojitos."

He responded, "YES!!!"

Laughing at his reply, I started to giggle like a child. I truly thought I had completely closed that chapter after we made beautiful love and left on such a great high. I was absolutely at peace with the way we left things, but maybe there was still something more. I didn't want to close the door now. I was feeling very excited to see him again---truth be told. This time it seemed as if the feelings of excitement were mutual between him and I.

I was going first to meet with Ada at one of my favorite places in Gràcia called Time Line. There I would gift her a framed picture of us over a cold and minty mojito. Memories flooded back to all the things we have done together here in Barcelona---stories of our dating life and me trying to play match maker on movie/picnic night at the castle in Montjuic or how one day we would both be on the Amazing Race together. It was a bittersweet goodbye.

However, mentally I couldn't help but feel the excitement building up to see Lucas soon. I think Ada could sense it as well.

I hugged Ada goodbye and was off to meet Lucas at the metro stop, Joanic. We gave each other a kiss and walked over to Gato Negro where my going away party took place. There he got to meet a few of my friends La Reina, Olen (Smiley), and Oscar. I told the story to Lucas how much they meant to me and how Smiley had

Larissa and me over for a proper Senegal dinner one evening. I still say one of the most amazing dishes I have ever had someone cook for me! So when I arrived for a final goodbye, they all gifted me a carved wooden guitar to take with me. Lucas could see the love I had for them and the love they had for me. He could see the life I was making without him unfold.

We continued through the night and went back to Lucas's place---same apartment, same bed, same place as when I first arrived in Barcelona. Wait, what???? Lucas, after our breakup, was able to get his old apartment back! There I was walking down the hallway to his bedroom with so many memories of the beginning of our story. Flashbacks started to flood my mind and heart. It suddenly hit me like a ton of bricks. I have always loved Lucas.

I was back in the bed where we first made love. This would also be the same bed where we would make love for the last time in Barcelona---my first and last love here as it was. This was such a full circle moment I could have never predicted.

Lucas always had a way of heightening all my sexual

desires. I fell in such a trance when he touched me. I never wanted a man sexually in every way the way I did with Lucas. Waking up the next day and in each other's arm, we chatted in bed about us and the unknown. We couldn't deny the feelings that were there but also not be oblivious to our separate paths at the moment with me heading back to Chicago and him back to Paris. I took one of Lucas's t-shirts for safe keeping that said *viente*. This translated to the word *wind* in English. Since Chicago is known as the Windy City and one of my personal favorite sayings is, "Go where the wind blows". I would give it back to him whenever he found me in Chicago again. Until then it was my turn to take a souvenir and a piece of him back with me as he did with me when we first met over two years ago by keeping a lock/strand of my hair in his wallet.

We left with a strong and passionate kiss that left me inebriated. We promised we would keep in contact with one another. I felt a sadness but also joy because of how happy I was for having shared a life with him, for having shared such a love I never had before, and for leaving with a forever friendship with him. "Lucas, thank you for making me want to be a better person, friend, and lover. I am better because of you."

I left knowing that my heart and ability to love was only deepen tenfold. Whether we got back together in the future or not I could give myself fully and wholly. I am so grateful for this extraordinary love with Lucas.

Chapter 30

I Finally Found What I Was Looking For

My last night in Barcelona I was having dinner with Katie and staying at her place before she took me and my over two hundred pounds of luggage to the airport the next day. I was looking forward to seeing her and recapping my eventful couple of days! There has always been a sense of peace whenever I would meet and catch up with Katie.

We went to a beautiful restaurant called Mirabe that overlooked the city of Barcelona. It was a magical spot that Katie recommended. I gave her that evening a framed picture of us as well as a keepsake. We both looked at each other with an overwhelming surrealness that I was actually leaving. Our friendship meant so much to me over the last couple of years. She had always been there for me from the beginning to the end. Our friendship had such a special and profound bond. The waiter came with our bottle of cold white Spanish wine named Viña Sol meaning: Sun Vineyard.

I thought to myself how poetic that my last bottle of wine was a sip of the sun. I mean my life had started in such darkness that I am now basking in the sunshine while sipping "the sun" and with every sip flows the happiest Annie to exist. I was me. I stopped living my life for what others said it should look like. I knew my life was just as good as the woman who had the perfect marriage on round one. I was whole, and I stopped dying inside but started to live! That bottle of wine was a gift from God, the universe as a loving message that I can end this chapter and head into a bright life.

Now, as I am sitting here on my flight from Barcelona to Chicago about to land in another hour or so I know a new chapter of my life is about to begin. I realized that sometimes the fairytale we have to have is the one we have with ourselves.

Pondering all the lessons I have learned in the past two years of my life went something like this:

- The universe will compel to give you what you want if you are willing to believe, take action, and not give up. Be brave.

- I am enough.

- I'm alive in every sense of the meaning! That in that definition meant that every vein in my breathing body is smiling with joy!

- The old wounds from my past, those unseen mental bruises, have finally diminished, and I am whole. I have purposely chosen that I am no longer a victim but the victor! I could finally look in the mirror and say I am beautiful, I am worth it, and I love you, Annie! I could love my invisible scars wholly.

- I forgive my past misfortunes. I forgive the men who once made me feel the complete opposite I do today. I am no longer allowing them to have any control whatsoever. I only wish good upon them.

- I love life. I mean truly LOVE life and know that the world is my oyster if I choose it to be.

- God/Universe is for me---not against me. There are times we don't understand the why, but I have learned everything is working in my favor even when it may not feel like it, and in that I give thanks always even when it's hard.

- The Law of Attraction is always working whether you want it to or not. I started teaching my conscious and my subconscious to realize the power of my thoughts. I am a walking magnet, and I must feed my mind the right things--- the greater the feeling the higher the vibrations that goes into the universe. Those vibrations are receiving a response EVERY single time. That's the power of manifesting.

- Having the ultimate freedom in my life now meant that other people's opinions of me just didn't matter. That my life didn't have to fit the status quo or match the others who society deems "did it the right way". Lady Gaga said it best, "Don't you ever let a soul in the world tell you that you can't be exactly who you are."

Flying thousands of feet in the air knowing that this girl has always been on a quest looking for that perfect love story. In the end I got it. I actually got it! The *Love Story* was never about finding the perfect partner but falling in love with me, THE ULTIMATE LOVE STORY!

A few months prior, Jeremiah and I had watched a movie called *Happy Thank You More Please* directed by Josh Radnor who also wrote the screenplay and is a main character in the movie. I thought he wrote it so brilliantly with such a deep message. Since having watched that movie now when I am feeling great or someone does something nice or whatever the case may be that creates that "feel good" feeling, I simply say to the universe, to God: "Thank you, more please!" Let me explain. I don't mean in a selfish greedy kind of way but in a way where I say, "WOW!", "Thank you!" "I would love more please." We ALL deserve to keep getting the "happy" whatever it is that makes you smile, brightens your heart a little more, and makes your day even better. So, I sit here about to land knowing how blessed my life has been in Barcelona and all the friends and experiences that have crossed my path that only made me better and more open minded, and I say to this new and upcoming chapter, I say to life, "Thank You! More please!"

Acknowledgments

Thank you to my mom for bringing me into this world. You are beautiful inside and out! I will always admire your heart more than you will ever know. I love you so very much!

Thank you to my dad for being an example of taking risks and chances. You came to America all on your own in your twenties without speaking any English but learned it! You exemplified courage that I, too, could go to another foreign country and learn another language. I will never forget the feeling I had when I came back to the USA and could speak to you in Spanish for the first time. I love you tons and tons!

Thank you to my sister and brother for going through life together as kids, even when it was hard for us all. I am grateful for you both, even if we did fight like cats and dogs! LOL, I love you both so much!

Thank you to my Aunt Barb for being there for me in my early twenties during a dark time in my life. You saved me more than you'll ever know. I love you!

Thank you to my dear friend Julie who rallied around my son and me when I returned to the U.S. You will never know how much that meant to me. I love you!

Thank you to Lisaette, my former coworker. You will never know how much I cherished our morning chats. The time I said I was going to make my book fictional, and you said no! I had to tell my story and be me. I am forever grateful for our paths crossing and our friendship. I love you!

Acknowledgments

Thank you, Barb, for bringing Kristy to brunch that Spring Sunday. Who knew she would be the one to introduce me to Rose Gold Publishing? I love you!

Thank you, Kristy, for the magic of that day at brunch in going with your heart to bring Dolly and me together. It has meant so much to me! I love you!

Thank you to Dolly; I mean, what can I say? Working with you, Rose Gold Publishing, has been beyond more than a dream. A friendship that I am beyond grateful for. You never cease to amaze me, and I just love you for it! I can't imagine working with anyone else for my first book. Simply Unapologetic. I love you!

Ryan, thank you for all your support and for loving the woman I have become. "I love you" isn't even enough to express the gratitude and love I have for you.

Finally, a huge thank you to God. You've never left my side through the darkness, yet you gave me light. Thank you always and forever. I love you so much!

About the Author

Annie L. Mendez is the founder of Atlas 2 Recreate, a Certified Life Coach, and the Author of Simply Unapologetic. Her passion began for writing when she was just five years old. Copying for hours her mom's hard covered green bible on a pad of paper. When she was ten years old, she wrote an essay with immense detail, heart, and soul. Her teacher gave her a failing grade and said, "No ten-year-old can write like this." Having a vision when she went to bed at twelve years old, she went to her principal the next day to inquire about starting their first ever newspaper called the Scammon Scoop. She was only twelve years old and became the editor and founder of her grammar schools first ever newspaper that is still going many years later today. She even had featured her own advice column.

Always knowing she was made for more. She began to contemplate on the trials in her life having gone through abuse. She wanted a voice for women to know that they could have a better life and recreate a life of their dreams. She discovered the Law of Attraction and began to religiously practice those teachings and ways of thinking to change her scenario.

Annie and her son moved to Barcelona, Spain (Catalunya) and she soon started to write her story in hopes of one day she would become a published author and help women from all around the world.

Today, Annie is continuing to live her dreams and travel the world! She has currently been to all seven continents and over eighty plus countries. Sharing her story and mission to help others know that they too can recreate a life they will love!

You may email Annie directly at Atlas2recreate@gmail.com or visit her website www.atlas2recreate.com.